HENRY
FONDA

HENRY FONDA

His Life and Work

Norm Goldstein

Michael Joseph • London

Off stage, 1955.

With special gratitude to:

The *Omaha World Herald*, The Omaha Community Playhouse, and The American Film Institute.

First published in Great Britain by Michael Joseph Ltd.
44 Bedford Square, London WC1   1982
Copyright © 1982 by the Associated Press

ISBN: 0 7181 2245 3
Printed and bound in the United States of America

Photo editor: Carol Deegan
"On the Broadway Stage" introduction: Jay Sharbutt
"On the Big Screen" introduction: Jay Arnold

ISBN 0-03-063353-2

HAN

Henry Fonda, 1938.

It was the summer of 1925, the midst of America's "Roaring Twenties" but not the best of times for the young man in suburban Dundee, Nebraska, outside Omaha.

The twenty-year-old had dropped out of the University of Minnesota after this, his sophomore year, and had come home to contemplate his future. He had decided not to return to school because working his way through college had proved to be too much. Classes at eight o'clock, then three to eleven at the Unity Settlement House, and sometimes weekend work for Northwestern Bell Telephone Company—it didn't even leave much time for his steady girl.

What he would do next was probably occupying his thoughts when his mother called him to the telephone.

"Do Brando's on the line," she said. "Just listen to her."

Dorothy "Do" Brando, although she had given birth to a son, Marlon, April 3, 1924, was again active with the Omaha Community Playhouse, where she was a member of the board of directors, a recruiter of talent, and a sometime-actress. Mrs. Brando, a neighbor and friend through the Christian Science church, was seeking a replacement for a young actor in *You and I,* a play by Philip Barry.

"We've lost our leading man," she said. "You'd be perfect for the part."

"Good God, Do," the youth replied. "I don't know how to act!"

But Do Brando was persuasive, and off the young man trudged into downtown Omaha to read the part of Ricky, the juvenile lead, before director Gregory Foley.

A genuine babe in the theatrical woods, he even read the stage directions! But he got the part, anyway.

"I was too self-conscious to say I didn't want to do it or I didn't know *how* to do it," Henry Jaynes Fonda was to recall years later. "I was so painfully introverted that I tucked the book under my arm, mumbled a few words, went home, and memorized the part."

Thus did Henry Fonda discover the "magic" of theater. He was hooked but good.

Acting quickly became his first and lasting love; indeed, his life.

In the next fifty-seven years, Henry Fonda was to appear in more than one hundred movies and plays, portraying cowboys and cabinet members, presidents and farmers, sailors and lawyers—but usually the decent, unspectacular hero; the symbol of the unbiased, uncorrupted American.

A consummate actor, a dignified professional, Fonda was able to convey deep and pervasive feelings to millions with what many critics saw as "captivating simplicity." A tall—six feet one—lean man with an honest face, he blended a distinctive, resonant midwestern drawl, a slight stoop, and a graceful, square-shouldered, purposeful stride into a perfection of style and grace.

The plays: *Mister Roberts, Point of No Return, The Caine Mutiny Court Martial, Generation, Clarence Darrow, First Monday in October.*

The films: *Young Mr. Lincoln, The Grapes of Wrath, The Ox-Bow Incident, My Darling Clementine, Mister Roberts, 12 Angry Men.* And, of course, *On Golden Pond.*

The television movies: "Gideon's Trumpet" (1979), "Summer Solstice" (1981).

Indeed, a stunning list of acting achievements, with a powerful scenario, full of triumphs and tears; for his private life as well. A naval officer, gentleman, medal winner, husband—five times, and father—two of his children, Jane and Peter, often taking the public spotlight from him.

Henry Fonda—an exceptional talent. An introverted, laconic man of few words, he could be aloof, cantankerous, and outwardly cool.

Author John Steinbeck, who had a strong friendship with Fonda for forty years, once made this assessment: "My impressions of Hank are of a man reaching but unreachable, gentle but capable of sudden wild and dangerous violence, sharply critical of others but equally self-critical, caged and fighting the bars but timid of the light, viciously opposed to external restraint, imposing an iron slavery on himself.

"His face is a picture of opposites in conflict."

If there were one constant in his life, however, it was his midwestern roots.

"I'm midwest and proud of it," he said. "I'm not asked, and I shouldn't be asked, to play Shakespeare or Restoration comedy classics, because I'm still Omaha, Nebraska. I've never tried hard to get away from that. When I have tried, I've felt phony."

Henry Fonda's Nebraska roots were planted in the prairie city of Grand Island, where he was born May 16, 1905. His parents, William Brace and Herberta Jaynes Fonda, had rented a house from banker George Bell in 1904 but lived there only six months before moving to Omaha, where William Fonda took a job as a printer.

Various sources say the Fondas were descended from a titled Italian who fled Genoa for The Netherlands centuries ago to escape political persecution. Some of his descendants founded the town of Fonda, New York—*almost* the birthplace of Henry Fonda.

The Grand Island house, a five-room wood structure, was later moved five miles from its downtown location to become part of the Stuhr Museum of the Prairie Pioneer. Fonda himself spent about $10,000 to move the house and pay for its restoration. It had to be pieced back together, as later owners had separated it into three apartments.

Fonda grew up with two younger sisters, Harriet (Mrs. M. J. "Zack" Warren), and the late Jayne Schoentgen, in Omaha and Dundee. Henry played baseball as a boy and became a boy scout, working up to eagle scout.

Two events of his childhood always stood out in his memory. The first was when he was five years old and his mother woke him up to see something quite special: Halley's comet, because "it comes around only once every seventy-six years."

The second, on September 28, 1919, was when his father took him downtown to watch the mob lynching of a young black man accused of raping a white woman. It was a chilling experience and profoundly influenced the teen-ager.

"I've never forgotten," Fonda said many years later. "My father didn't preach about it, didn't say anything about hatred. He didn't need to."

After graduating from Omaha Central High School in 1923, Fonda decided to take a crack at journalism and entered the University of Minnesota. One reason for the move to Minneapolis was that Northwestern Bell had an office there and he could work his way through school.

But he exhausted himself working at the settlement house and occasionally as a trouble-shooter for the phone company and was back in Omaha when Do Brando called.

Long after Henry Fonda had reached the peak of his profession, he remembered those beginnings:

"I was so shy that I'd been cast, and weeks had gone by before I tried to say, 'You can't do this to me,'" he said of his first time on stage at the Omaha Community Playhouse. "Three years later, I'd heard you could get money for this. So I came to New York with a hundred dollars in my pocket.

"The folks back home thought I was so daring. But it had nothing to do with guts. I didn't know what I was getting into. I don't know what I'd have done if I had known."

But once "Do Brando had, more or less, nudged me on to the stage of the Omaha Community Playhouse . . . I discovered this magic of theater that I had never known anything about. For the whole eight months of that first season, I was totally involved with all the many jobs that are around a little theater. Building and painting scenery and hanging lights and pulling the curtain up."

It was a great cure for his supreme shyness, too.

"I liked the feeling of being up there after I realized that all eyes were not on me all the time. I lost most of my self-consciousness and began to relax. It took me three years to decide that maybe this was what I really wanted to do."

At the end of his first season at the playhouse, though, his father decided it was probably time the young man thought seriously about making a living instead of playing around on stage. So Hank Fonda got a job as a file clerk at the Retail Credit Company.

Three months later, director Greg Foley called and offered him the lead role in *Merton of the Movies*.

"When I announced this at home, my dad was appalled. And he made it very clear that it was a lot of nonsense. I had a good job, it was a chance for advancement, and he wasn't going to dream of letting me jeopardize this.

"Well, we had quite a fierce argument until my mother stepped in as a mediator. And I kept the job and I rehearsed *Merton* evenings and weekends. I didn't see my father a great deal during those weeks. When we did meet, he gave me the silent treatment. It was a towering silence. And the message was clear: that once I forgot this foolishness and concentrated on a business career, he would resume communication.

"Merton is a young grocery clerk in a small town who kneels beside his cot every night and prays that God will make him a big movie star. Are you ready for that?

"We had the opening night, and the family did come, and my sister Harriet came back to the dressing room afterwards and said that the family would wait for me at home. And I finally got home, and I came in the house, and dad was sitting in his chair behind his newspaper. So I joined my mother and my sisters, who immediately tried to outdo each other with superlatives until Harriet began to say something that sounded as though it might become a criticism.

"And dad's paper came down, and he said, 'Shut up! He was perfect!'

"That's the best notice I ever got."

Fonda (far right), with friends in Omaha, about 1913.

But Henry Fonda wasn't ready to commit himself to acting—yet.

In an interview during the run of *Merton* in 1926, he told his Central High School newspaper, the *Register*, "I don't intend to make acting my profession; it is just my hobby. It was thrilling at first, but the glamour has worn off. From 7:30 a.m. to 7:30 p.m., I am a businessman."

Still, the young Fonda remained at the Omaha Community Playhouse as assistant director (including janitorial duties!) on and off for three years at $500 per year, meanwhile supporting himself with temporary jobs as iceman, window dresser, garage mechanic, and working for the Retail Credit Company.

But he found out something important about his acting.

"I discovered that it was therapy for a self-conscious young man and I could put on a mask—hide behind it—and pretend to be this brilliant man—clever, witty fellow—that the playwright had conceived."

It was far more than therapy. On that Omaha stage, some thirteen hundred miles from Broadway, more than sixteen hundred miles from Hollywood, Henry Fonda experienced a sensation, almost a palpable euphoria, that wedded him to the stage forever. It was a feeling he never forgot, and it brought him back to the theater time and again.

"The short hair on the back of my neck felt like live wires, and my skin tingled. This was the first time I realized what acting meant."

Now it was time to find out if he could get paid for this foolishness. He went East.

He tried New York to no avail. Jobs—any jobs—were tough to come by, but he heard about summer theaters in New England and knocked on stage doors in the Cape Cod area, finally landing pittance-paying work as "third assistant stage manager" and, eventually, bit roles.

Provincetown, Dennis, Falmouth—small-town playhouses with promising talents from nearby schools. Some of these talents had joined together in the University Players, a group of mostly college students sharpening their theatrical skills.

The University Players opened in Falmouth on July 9, 1928. Soon after, an Omaha friend, Bernard Hanighen, who was doing some unfinished school work at Harvard, brought Fonda over there from Dennis to see a play, George Kelly's comedy *The Torch-bearers*, about amateur theatricals in Philadelphia. Joshua Logan played the part of Huxley Hossefrosse, developing what he called a "human capon" voice for the role.

In his autobiography, Logan recalls:

"At the second performance, the moment I spoke my first line a high, strangulated sob came from the darkness. I thought someone was having an asthmatic attack. I said my second line and the wail came out again, higher and flatter this time. Some odd human animal out there found me funny. And, to my delight, it was infecting the audience. . . ."

After the performance, Hanighen brought Fonda backstage to introduce him to Logan.

"This is my friend, Hank Fonda."

"Standing in the doorway," Logan remembered, "was a tall, lean man in his early twenties. His head jutted forward over a concave chest and a protruding abdomen which made him seem to lead with his crotch. He wore skimpy, white plus four knickers, long black socks and black shoes. Either he had a daring tailor or he just didn't care. I was to find out the latter. His extraordinarily handsome, almost beautiful face and huge innocent eyes, combined with that rough hewn physique, made for a startling effect.

"He was looking at me as though he were about to pop. 'You were Huxley Hossefrosse, weren't you?'

"'Yes,' I answered, and he exploded with that same strangled sob laugh I'd heard all evening. At that moment I knew I would care for him the rest of my life."

Others in the troupe included a young and beautiful Virginia belle, Margaret Sullavan, Kent Smith, Elizabeth Fenner, Myron McCormick, and, later, Mildred Natwick and a young Princetonian named Jimmy Stewart.

The association produced friendships that were to last a lifetime.

The University Players changed from a repertory company, with different plays and roles every night, to a stock company, running a play a full week and then taking it on the road.

They played *Death Takes a Holiday* (Death, on a holiday, visits an Italian family and falls in love with the beautiful daughter) in Baltimore, with Fonda and Kent Smith playing opposite Miss Sullavan. Fonda and the beautiful "Peggy" became favorites of the Maryland city; crowds waited for autographs, and newspapers wrote about their romantic lives. It seemed the stage romance carried on off-stage as well.

On Christmas Day, 1931, at noon, the acting company gathered in the large, dreary dining room of the Kernan Hotel and witnessed the marriage of Henry Fonda and Margaret Sullavan.

The arrangement lasted a matter of four months. Tempers and temperaments clashed; "squabbles" became screaming arguments. With several Broadway hits behind her, Margaret Sullavan's career was soaring; Henry Fonda's was as yet unsung. They agreed to part, without bitterness.

Fonda left the University Players and went out on his own. "He was a tremendous loss," said Logan. "He was the heart of the company."

He moved into a run-down apartment on West 64th Street off Central Park West in Manhattan, rooming with Logan, McCormick, and Stewart. He was broke, out of work, living on a box of rice, but having a good time, too.

Actress Margaret Sullavan, Fonda's first wife, as she appeared in a 1937 publicity photo.

Henry Fonda, with Dorothy McGuire (age thirteen) and George McIntyre, in *A Kiss for Cinderella* at the Omaha Community Playhouse.

In their "soot-colored bedroom with twin beds," they laughed, drank, listened to good jazz—and rotated sleeping arrangements so as to leave the living-room couches to those who had dates. Stewart played the accordion, and Fonda showed off another talent—he could walk on his hands. He also managed bit roles on Broadway; his first was as walk-on and understudy in *A Game of Life and Death*, with Alice Brady, Claude Rains, and Otto Kruger.

During those struggles to get a start on Broadway, he jumped at a chance to return to Omaha. Greg Foley had persuaded him to "guest star" in a play of his own choosing. He picked *A Kiss for Cinderella,* since he had played it with Margaret Sullavan in Falmouth and with Mildred Natwick in a Children's Theater production in Washington.

To play opposite him, he selected a thirteen-year-old from Omaha—Dorothy McGuire.

In the summer of 1932, the only job he could get was driving a station wagon for a stock company in Surrey, New Hampshire. In the middle of the season, he took over—as set designer. And a good one, too.

"The next summer," he once recalled, "I couldn't get arrested as an actor—but I had the pick of every theater in the country to do settings."

He chose to do settings at the Westchester Theater in Mt. Kisco, New York, because it was near Manhattan—and Broadway.

"There was an open week in the middle of the summer, and the producer asked me if I knew of a simple five-role play." Fonda suggested *It's A Wise Child,* because "I'd done it with the University Players and said I could do the small iceman role in it and save the producer an actor's salary. The part had just one scene in the first act and another in the third—but it was the role everyone went home remembering."

Among those who remembered was an actress named June Walker. She was later to bring him to Broadway for a role that would change his life.

"If I hadn't gone to Surrey that summer . . ."

Meanwhile, Fonda landed a part in the first edition of Leonard Sillman's *New Faces* of 1934, in which he showed a flair for comedy, doing some stints with a young lady who only wanted to be a dancer, Imogene Coca. That association extended off-stage in a brief affair with the lady Fonda described as "an adorable little clown—with so much talent."

Among those who enjoyed *New Faces* was a theatrical agent named Leland Hayward, who immediately signed Fonda to a contract. Soon after, while Fonda was playing leads at the summer theater in Westchester, Hayward telephoned from California. He wanted Fonda to come out to the West Coast to be in the movies.

Fonda's answer was typically terse: "No."

But Hayward persisted.

"I'll pay your fare out here. Come and just spend the day."

He sent him a plane ticket and met him at the Burbank airport.

Fonda was introduced to producer Walter Wanger and signed to do two pictures in a year—at $1,000 a week!

But there was no picture available at the time, so Fonda returned to Westchester and played in *The Swan* and then in Marc Connelly's *The Farmer Takes a Wife*.

In *The Swan,* Fonda played the tutor opposite Geoffrey Kerr, who was the prince in the Molnar story about a princess and a commoner in love. It was Kerr's wife, June Walker—she had seen Fonda in Surrey—who recommended him to costar with her in the new play by Connelly.

Fonda read for the title lead in *The Farmer Takes a Wife* and was happily hired by Connelly and producer Max Gordon for a run-of-the-play contract at $225 a week.

It all seemed to be coming together for Fonda when his mother, Herberta, died.

"It was a cruel blow," Fonda told biographer Howard Teichmann, "and I felt so badly that she didn't live to see me move ahead."

The Farmer Takes a Wife, by Connelly and Frank P. Elser, is a comedy dealing with life along the Erie Canal. It—and Fonda—got superb reviews in its opening efforts in Washington, D.C., and again at Broadway's 46th Street Theatre.

When 1935 dawned, Henry Fonda was still living at the Madison Square Hotel with roommate Jimmy Stewart but was at the top of his new-found Broadway world. *Farmer* ran more than one hundred performances before closing.

Twentieth Century-Fox had bought screen rights to the play as a vehicle for Janet Gaynor. They wanted Fonda to recreate his role on screen but learned he was under contract to Wanger. They considered Gary Cooper and Joel McCrea. But, finally, Fox arranged a deal to borrow Fonda for the film.

Victor Fleming, director of the film version (he was later to direct *Gone with the Wind*), was able to teach the neophyte film actor what Fonda later described as "the biggest message I ever got in Hollywood"—how to pull down a performance for the more intimate movie medium.

"I just pulled it right back to reality," Fonda told biographer Teichmann, "because that lens and that microphone are doing all the projection you need. No sense in using too much voice, and you don't need any more expression on your face than you'd use in everyday life."

When the movie opened at Radio City Music Hall in August 1935, *New York Times* film critic Andre Sennwald, noting "the sentimental warmth and the

This group of talented young actors and actresses called themselves the University Players when they appeared in various productions in Baltimore, Maryland, in the early 1930s. Here they are seen in Philip Barry's play *Holiday*, which was staged at the Maryland Theater in 1932. Left to right are Henry Fonda, Myron McCormick, Margaret Sullavan, Joshua Logan, and Barbara O'Neil. Fonda and Miss Sullavan had wed several weeks earlier, on December 24, 1931.

pungent charm of the most lovable of recent American folk plays," made special mention of the newcomer to Hollywood:

"Mr. Fonda in his film debut is the biggest particular star of the occasion. As the virtuous farm boy, he played with an immensely winning simplicity which will make him one of our most attractive actors."

Although his second film, *Way Down East*, a remake of the silent movie, did not fare nearly as well, Sennwald noted that it was a "personal triumph" for the young leading man.

Jimmy Stewart had come out to Hollywood, for M-G-M, and he and Fonda renewed their living arrangements, with the addition of a cat named George. John Swope, another graduate of the University Players days, joined them.

Fonda and Stewart shared some Hollywood night life, too. One night they double-dated; Stewart was paired with Ginger Rogers, and Fonda escorted Lucille Ball. They went dancing at the Coconut Grove and ended up at dawn in Barney's Beanerie, where Stewart commented that the women's makeup looked heavy in the morning light. Fonda agreed, and the evening's ardor was quickly cooled.

"If I'd behaved myself," Fonda was to joke later, "they might have named that studio Henrylu, not Desilu."

Margaret Sullavan had come out West, too. She was now remarried, to film director William Wyler. Josh Logan joined the old group, too.

Fonda followed *Way Down East* with *I Dream Too Much*, with Lily Pons, and *The Trail of the Lonesome Pine*—the first outdoor Western in Technicolor—in which he played a hillbilly, which may have inspired much of Al Capp's "Li'l Abner" cartoon character. He costarred with ex-wife Margaret Sullavan (then separated from Wyler) in a frothy comedy called *The Moon's Our Home* and then a B picture called *Spendthrift*.

In the summer of 1936, Fonda sailed to England to join the French actress Annabella in *Wings of the Morning*. (It was the first Technicolor picture in England.) While on the set in Denham Studios, Henry Fonda met Frances Seymour Brokaw.

The tall, aristocratic Frances Seymour had married multimillionaire George Brokaw, who died earlier that year. Brokaw left a socially prominent and wealthy widow and a daughter, Pamela (although she was called Pan, short for Panchita, Spanish for Frances). Frances Brokaw and Henry Fonda hit it off immediately in London and traveled together to Berlin, Munich, and Budapest.

He proposed marriage to her in Budapest. She accepted in Paris. They married in New York, at Christ Church, September 16, 1936.

Joshua Logan was best man; Leland Hayward one of the ushers.

On December 21, 1937, Frances gave birth to Jane Seymour Fonda; Peter Henry Fonda was born February 23, 1939.

Opposite: Newlyweds Henry and Frances Fonda about to depart on a flight to Omaha, Nebraska, shortly after their wedding. (*Inset*) Henry and Frances as they board a train from New York to California in February 1938. In the basket is their infant daughter, Jane, born December 21, 1937.

Henry Fonda and Frances Seymour Brokaw on September 16, 1936, their wedding day. It was the second marriage for both.

Meanwhile, Fonda kept working, acting in a series of efforts of varied quality, beginning with *You Only Live Once*, a Fritz Lang film with Sylvia Sidney, and *Slim*, with Pat O'Brien. Years later, when Fonda listed his favorite films, the well-known ones were there, with the surprising addition of *Slim*—"a very good film that was overlooked," he said.

He played opposite Bette Davis in *Jezebel*; then in *The Mad Miss Manton*, with Barbara Stanwyck. And he played Mr. Watson to Don Ameche's Alexander Graham Bell in the film biography of the inventor *The Story of Alexander Graham Bell*.

He also returned—as always—to the theater: Broadway for *Blow Ye Winds* (1937) and summer theaters for *The Virginian*. Then, in 1939, he was offered a role that remains one of the star efforts in the Fonda galaxy.

For a biography of John Ford, Fonda recalled how it came about:

"They had sent me the script and I told them, 'Forget it. I can't play Lincoln.' I sent it back. But [studio boss] Darryl Zanuck and [writer] Lamar Trotti kept after me, and finally I agreed to make a test. A few days later we screened it, and when I saw this big tall character up there with the big nose, the hair, the wart and everything, it just didn't seem right.

"'No way,' I said. 'I am not going to play Abraham Lincoln.'

"In the meantime, Pappy Ford had been assigned to the picture. I had never met him, but I admired his work for years. He called me into his office. He was sitting behind a desk with a hat pulled down over his eyes, and was chomping on a pipe and a handkerchief all at the same time. He looked at me for a long while. I remember feeling like a sailor, a bluejacket, standing in front of an admiral. I didn't know how I was going to explain that I just couldn't play Lincoln.

"Suddenly, he sprang up and said, 'What's all this bullshit about you not wanting to play Abraham Lincoln? You're playing a jacklegged lawyer from Springfield, Illinois, a gawky kid still wet behind the ears who rides a mule because he can't afford a horse.'

"I couldn't believe it. How could he talk about Abraham Lincoln in such a way? But he was right. He was asking me to see the character for what he was. I had him on too high a pedestal, and he was shaming me into playing him."

Young Mr. Lincoln started shooting in February 1939 and opened a year later. By that time, Ford and Fonda were partnered again, shooting *Drums Along the Mohawk* at a remote location in Utah's Wasatch Range.

Young Mr. Lincoln opened at New York's Roxy Theater to outstanding reviews. "Henry Fonda's characterization is one of those once-in-a-blue-moon things: a crossroads meeting of nature, art and a smart casting director," wrote critic Frank Nugent.

Nature gave Mr. Fonda long arms and legs, a strong and honest face and a slow smile; the make-up man added a new

Opposite: Fonda in a 1939 publicity photo.

Fonda as he appears the same year in *Young Mr. Lincoln* for Twentieth Century-Fox, 1939.

nose bridge, the lank brown hair, the frock coat and stove-pipe hat (the beard hadn't begun to sprout in those days) and the trace of a mole.

Mr. Fonda supplied the rest—the warmth and kindliness, the pleasant modesty, the courage, resolution, tenderness, shrewdness and wit that Lincoln, even young Mr. Lincoln, must have possessed. His performance kindles the film, makes it a moving unity, at once gentle and quizzically comic.

While shooting *Drums Along the Mohawk*, Darryl Zanuck offered Ford and Fonda the movie that many believe was written for Fonda: *The Grapes of Wrath*, from John Steinbeck's powerful Pulitzer Prize-winning novel about itinerant Okie farmers in Dust Bowl Depression days.

Fonda was a great admirer of Steinbeck's and jumped at the chance to play Tom Joad. After taking a month off, Ford agreed, too. Jane Darwell was signed to play Ma Joad; John Carradine the defrocked priest; Russell Simpson was Pa Joad, and Charles Grapewin Grandpa Joad. All were Fox contract players at the time. Nunnally Johnson adapted the book to the screen, and it began shooting in the San Fernando Valley in September.

It is a classic film, topped by the extraordinary performance by Henry Fonda as the tough, simple, straightforward son of the American heartland, driven through his sense of justice to social commitment.

Fonda once recalled shooting the scene in which he says good-by to Ma Joad at the government camp:

"The shot started inside the tent. I go in, shake her and whisper that I want to talk to her, then go out and wait until she puts on a robe. She comes out, and we walk around and sit on this dance floor where they've had a dance the night before. We don't go into our dialogue until we sit down.

"Most directors would have shot this scene in two or three different setups. But Pappy wanted to do it all in one shot. That made it technically difficult because it meant that the camera had to be mounted on a track and they had to pull back from the tent, then dolly over to the bench with it.

"We rehearsed it and rehearsed it so that the camera crew could get the moves down. Every time we got to the bench and were about to go into our lines, Pappy would say, 'Cut.' He didn't make a big deal out of it; he just said, 'Cut.' Well, as actors we were very much aware of the emotion in this scene, and we really wanted to run it. We were like race horses chomping at the bit, but he wouldn't let us go until the camera was ready. When we finally did run the scene we were ready! I mean, the emotion was built up inside of us, and it was working for us.

"It was there in the face and in the eyes, and we had to fight to hold it back. It was a great, great scene, and we knew it right then."

Others found out when it opened at the Rivoli Theatre in New York in January 1940. The *New York Times*, noting that Fonda played his character just the way Steinbeck had in mind, "hot-tempered, resolute, saturnine," added:

In the vast library where the celluloid literature of the screen is stored, there is one small uncrowded shelf devoted to the cinema's masterworks, to those films, which by dignity of theme and excellence of treatment, seem destined to be recalled not merely at the end of their particular year, but whenever great motion pictures are mentioned.

To that shelf of screen classics, Twentieth Century-Fox added its version of John Steinbeck's *Grapes of Wrath*. . . .

The Grapes of Wrath earned Academy Awards for John Ford's direction and Jane Darwell's acting. Fonda's performance was nominated, competing with that of Jimmy Stewart in *Philadelphia Story*, Charlie Chaplin in *The Great Dictator*, Raymond Massey in *Abe Lincoln in Illinois*, and Laurence Olivier in *Rebecca*.

Fonda never believed in the Oscars; he felt it was impossible to compare performances in different roles. So he didn't seem to be deeply disappointed in not getting that Oscar, especially when the winner was his buddy Jimmy Stewart.

There was some disappointment, however, in being persuaded by Zanuck to sign a contract with Fox. (Wanger had disbanded his studio.) Zanuck had drawn him into the contract waters by dangling the Tom Joad role as bait. He almost drowned in it, forced to play in some less-than memorable films like *Lillian Russell* (with Alice Faye and nine other male costars) and *The Magnificent Dope*.

On a "loan-out" to Paramount, however, it was a different story. Fonda teamed with Barbara Stanwyck in *The Lady Eve*, the Preston Sturges comedy in which Fonda was a girl-shy millionaire. He had played opposite Miss Stanwyck before, in *The Mad Miss Manton*, but "I fell in love with Barbara when we did *Lady Eve*," Fonda said. "She's a delicious woman. We've never had an affair—she's never encouraged me."

One other film in this prewar period, *The Male Animal*, (with Olivia De Havilland) worked out well for him, playing the young professor who defies football-crazed trustees by reading his students a letter written by Vanzetti to Sacco. (It was to be redone in 1952 as *She's Working Her Way Through College*, with Ronald Reagan in the Fonda role.)

In another disagreement with Zanuck, Fonda fought to do a film about lynch-mob violence in 1885 Nevada—*The Ox-Bow Incident*. Zanuck didn't see much box-office appeal in that theme, but Fonda, along with director William Wellman and producer-writer Lamar Trotti, won out.

It is one of Fonda's finer film roles and surely recalled for him the embedded images of the lynching his father had taken him to witness more than twenty years earlier. (Interestingly, there is a similar theme in Fonda's *Young Mr. Lincoln* in which he argues: "If those boys had more than one life, I'd say, 'Go ahead. Maybe a little hanging mightn't do 'em any harm. But the sort of hanging you boys'd give 'em would be so—so permanent. Trouble is when men start taking the law into their own hands, they're just as apt—in all the confusion and fun—to start hanging somebody who's not a murderer as somebody who is.'")

Ox-Bow was touted by critics as "hard to beat for sheer, stark drama," with Fonda "cryptic and bitter as one of the stauncher holdouts for justice." But the film was a box-office failure, though it is still popular in re-issues.

At home, the Fondas had found their dream property in what is now Bel-Air, California, and built the place called Tigertail, much like a Pennsylvania Dutch farmhouse. Frances had handled most of the financial arrangements. As business dealings seemed to pre-occupy her more and more, her health seemed to be suffering as well. She visited doctors often and

checked into the Scripps Clinic for several weeks.

Meanwhile, 600 Tigertail Road took shape. An outside pool looked like an old swimmin' hole. A smaller building, the playhouse, was usually occupied by the children. Fonda took to gardening seriously. He bought a horse for Pan and a stable to house it. Later, he got two burros for Jane and Peter.

Then came December 7, 1941, and the war. Henry Fonda registered for the draft right away.

One night, he and Frances talked about taking the next step. Fonda recalled the conversation to biographer Teichmann:

"The Navy?" Frances asked.
"That's it."
"But you're exempt. . . . You have three dependents. Why, Hank?"

One of the last shots of Fonda prior to his military service.

I looked down from our bridge and saw our captain's palm tree! Our trophy for superior achievement! The Admiral John J. Finchley Award for delivering more toothpaste and toilet paper than any other Navy cargo ship in the safe area of the Pacific.

As Lt. Doug Roberts in *Mister Roberts*

Henry Fonda, thirty-seven, enlists in the navy as an apprentice seaman on August 24, 1942.

He reports for duty on
November 18, 1942, in Los
Angeles.

I've discovered, doc, that the unseen enemy of this war is the boredom that eventually becomes a faith and, therefore, a terrible sort of suicide—and I know now that the ones who refuse to surrender to it are the strongest of all.

Ensign Pulver reading a last letter from Mr. Roberts in *Mister Roberts*

Order of the Palm. To Lt. (j.g.) Douglas Roberts for action against the enemy, above and beyond the call of duty.

From the crew, for throwing "that damn palm tree" overboard

Still in uniform, Fonda is shown here with his wife, Frances, during an evening at the Stork Club in New York (1945).

Back to being an actor, 1946.

". . . the wives and mothers of a lot of soldiers and sailors'll see me on screen and say, 'Why isn't he out there?' "

"What about the picture you're shooting [The Ox-Bow Incident]?"

"It'll end soon enough. Frances, I don't want to do any more movies. I don't want to sell war bonds or be photographed with soldiers and sailors. I want to *be* a sailor."

"Duty?"

"You said it. I didn't."

"Patriotism?"

"Frances, this is my country and I want to be where it's happening. I don't want to be in a fake war in a studio or on location. I'm not crazy about the idea of getting hurt, but I want to be on a real ocean not the back lot. I want to be with real sailors not extras."

"In other words . . . you want the genuine article."

"That's about it."

On August 24, 1942, the day after he finished shooting *The Ox-Bow Incident*, Henry Fonda, thirty-seven years old, drove to Naval Headquarters in downtown Los Angeles and without one bit of ballyhoo became Henry Fonda, apprentice seaman, the navy's lowest billing.

"I'd like to be with the fellows who handle the guns," he said.

Fox studio publicity personnel said they were entirely unaware that he had planned to enlist. (On the same day, in Washington, Tyrone Power, Fonda's friend and colleague, enlisted as a private in the marines, taking the oath before a mob of cameramen and reporters.) But Darryl Zanuck didn't give up one of his stars that easily. He pulled some strings and got Fonda out of boot camp in San Diego to do a quick war propaganda film, *The Immortal Sergeant*.

Then Henry Fonda went to the real war. He went to quartermaster school and was assigned to the destroyer the U.S.S. *Satterlee* as a qualified signalman third class. He was later commissioned as a lieutenant junior grade and ordered to the Navy Department in Washington to make training films. But that was not the real war Fonda had opted for, and he asked instead for active duty. He got it.

He was transferred to a destroyer, assigned to the staff of Vice Adm. John H. Hoover, who served directly under Fleet Adm. Chester Nimitz, U.S. naval commander in the Pacific. Fonda served well and received a Bronze Star and presidential citation for his work as an operations and air-combat intelligence officer when he was discharged as a lieutenant senior grade in October 1945.

It was party time on his return, parties and pleasure and gardening at Tigertail. Friend Jimmy Stewart called it "our kite-building period."

Pappy Ford got him back into the movie business with a realistic and exciting Western centered on the frontier marshal of Tombstone, Wyatt Earp. In *My Darling Clementine*, Fonda plays an unconventional Earp—heavily moustached, grizzled, slouching.

Critic Bosley Crowther wrote: "Henry Fonda, through his quiet, yet persuasive self-confidence—his delicious intonation of short words—shows us an elemental character who is as real as the dirt on which he walks."

In the next few years after *Clementine*, Fonda filmed *The Long Night* for Anatole Litvak and *The Fugitive* for Ford, an attempt to deal with the "whiskey priest" characterization of Graham Greene's *Power and the Glory*. Neither was successful.

Daisy Kenyon, a soap opera of a film with Joan Crawford, was the last movie he made under his Fox contract, in 1948. Another John Ford Western, *Fort Apache*, was the last film he was to make for seven years. He seemed to require the restorative powers of the stage, a live audience—and a substantive part.

Josh Logan called. He and Tom Heggen had a new play, and both thought of Henry Fonda.

"I asked Hank by wire if I could read him the play one afternoon," Logan recounts in his autobiography *Josh*.

I told him I knew he wasn't free, but he should hear it. He agreed . . .

As another possibility, I had thought that perhaps the actor . . . should be someone close in type to Tom Heggen himself—a small, unobtrusive man rather than the big, handsome hero type—and so I asked David Wayne, so great in *Finian's Rainbow*, if he would attend the reading too. I told Wayne, "Fonda's not free to play this part, so you mustn't think you're second choice."

"With Fonda, I like being second choice."

With Tom at my side, wincing, I read the play to Hank and David. The second I finished, David, who had not changed his expression throughout, charged out of the room. The rest of us looked at each other and shrugged. I turned to Hank, "Hank, I'm really sorry you can't play this role."

"Don't be sorry. I'm going to play it," he said.

"But the [movie] contract? You've signed it. . . ."

"My agent, Lew Wasserman, is supposed to be a powerhouse. I'll just tell him to get me out of that picture because I'm going to play Doug Roberts."

. . . Within minutes, the phone rang. It was David Wayne. "Hank Fonda should play Roberts, not me. I want to play Pulver. In fact, I've got to!"

Thus, Henry Fonda began the role he was to be identified with throughout his career, throughout his life, a role that was surely his favorite and closest to him.

Mister Roberts is about the crew of the broken-down cargo ship, the *Reluctant*, shuttling "from Apathy to Tedium with occasional side trips to Monotony." Mr. Roberts is the executive officer who is eager to be transferred to the war zone.

There was only one woman in the stage cast, a nurse. Eva Marie Saint was set to play the role, but she seemed "too attractive" to Logan and producer Leland Hayward. Fonda came up with a "Nebraska connection."

He telephoned a girl from Omaha, one whose family he knew well. Jocelyn Brando got the part.

Public reception of *Mister Roberts*, beginning in February 1949, was the stuff acting dreams are made of. Standing ovations. Curtain calls. One critic said he waited a long while after the final curtain, "hoping they would do it again."

The dean of theatrical critics at the time, Brooks Atkinson, of the *New York Times*, said:

Now that Mr. Fonda is back after eleven years, it would be nice to have him back for good. He has brought quite a lot of good with him this time. As Roberts, he is lanky and unheroic, relaxed and genuine; he neatly skirts the maudlin when the play grows sentimental, and he skillfully underplays the bombastic scenes.

"A royal good time," he concluded.
"A perfect human performance," he was to write in recollecting the opening once again.

It is difficult to define the perfection of Mr. Fonda's acting. . . . simple and genuine . . . not a trace of the exhibitionism of a Hollywood film star returning to Broadway. You are hardly aware Mr. Fonda is acting at all.
But he must be, for Mr. Roberts is a fully-drawn character, obsessed with one idea that seems reasonable and admirable.

The euphoria of his acting apex was sadly juxtaposed with life at home. Frances had set up the bedroom as a business office, telephones on both sides of the bed, ledgers and date books scattered about.
"I thought to myself," Fonda reported to Teichmann, "'Is this what my marriage comes down to?' Many days I'd blame myself. Then I hinted maybe she ought to see a doctor or two."
She did, and while Fonda was away, she underwent a hysterectomy. But her illness, to many, seemed more neurotic than physical. She became more and more withdrawn, sad and lethargic. She entered sanitariums for weeks at a time.
Then Henry Fonda met someone else, Oscar Hammerstein's stepdaughter, Susan Blanchard. He told Frances he wanted a divorce. She seemed to accept it with sympathy and understanding.
Plans were made for the divorce. Frances changed her will to cut out Henry Fonda completely.
Frances suffered a complete nervous breakdown and

Opposite: Once again at the Stork Club, Fonda joins fellow actors James Stewart, center, and Charles Boyer, at right, in 1948, while starring in *Mister Roberts* on Broadway.

Fonda getting ready to play *Mister Roberts* at New York's Alvin Theatre.

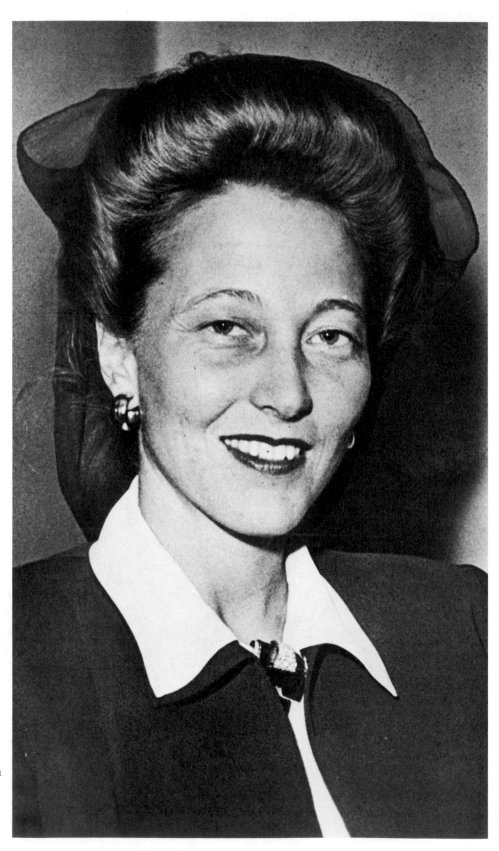

Henry Fonda's second wife, Frances Seymour Brokaw, the mother of his children, Jane and Peter, committed suicide on April 14, 1950, while in an up-state New York sanitarium she had entered after suffering a nervous breakdown.

went back into a sanitarium in Massachusetts, then later to the Craig House in Beacon, New York, near her mother.

On April 14, 1950, Frances Seymour Brokaw Fonda, forty-two years old, killed herself by slashing her throat with a razor blade.

She had been at Craig since February. She left a note in which Assistant D.A. Edward Russell quoted her as saying suicide "was the best way out." She was found dying in a sanitarium bathroom. The night nurse had entered her room with a glass of orange juice, the bed was empty, and there was a note on the floor: "Do not enter the bathroom but call Dr. Bennett."

The nurse called Dr. Courtney Bennett, staff physician, who entered the bathroom and found her bleeding on the floor, a razor blade nearby. She died in a matter of minutes.

Fonda hurried to Beacon for the funeral service and cremation, then returned to New York to go on stage for the 883rd performance of Mister Roberts.

"It was the only way I could get through the evening," he said.

The children were told that their mother had died of a heart attack. How that affected their lives is a question best left to psychiatry.

Nine months later, on January 6, 1951, ten-year-old Peter, at his grandmother's house in Katonah, near Ossining, New York, was wounded seriously by the accidental discharge of a .22-caliber pistol that went off while he was loading it. The bullet entered his stomach and lodged in his back. It was nearly fatal.

Peter made a quick and "amazing" comeback, however, as Henry flew to his side from the Virgin Islands, where he and twenty-two-year-old Susan Blanchard, married on December 28, 1950, were spending their honeymoon.

Peter spent a month in the hospital and a month at home recuperating.

Henry went back to Mister Roberts, taking the play on tour to Pittsburgh, Cleveland, Columbus, Cincinnati, Madison, Des Moines, Minneapolis, and, of course, Omaha.

Finally, in the summer of 1951, it was time to get discharged from Mister Roberts. After Fonda's last performance, Josh Logan told him enthusiastically, "You were better tonight than when you opened."

It was, perhaps, the finest compliment for Fonda, who felt that "anyone who gives the same performance he gave on opening night is not doing a good job. Unless a performance is growing constantly, unless the actor is finding new insights into the character, he must grow stale."

Growing stale was not a problem that Fonda ever had.

Leland Hayward, Fonda's agent and producer of Mister Roberts—who became Margaret Sullavan's third husband—had another play for Fonda. After the children were ensconced in Eastern boarding schools, Jane at Emma Willard in Troy, New York, and Peter at

the Fay School in Massachusetts, Fonda invested some of his own money and starred with Leora Dana in Point of No Return.

He followed that success with one of his most difficult, and most satisfying, stage roles, that of Barney Greenwald, the reluctant defense lawyer in The Caine Mutiny Court Martial. In the final Caine scene—Fonda called it the toughest he had as yet played—he has to follow an emotional climax with "a spirit-stirring second layer."

"Techniques aren't enough then," Fonda said at the time. "I have to become emotionally involved. I know I'm able to do it most of the time. I can feel it, and so can the audience.

"It's the difference between them saying, 'Well, Fonda was good, all right,' and the performances when they cheer and yell, 'Bravo,' for the whole company."

Critics marveled at the way he was able to "underplay" the role, an assessment of his acting that he heard throughout his career.

"I don't understand honestly what people mean when they say I underplay roles," he once told AP drama critic Bill Glover. "What I try to do is to be so real in a part that the audience doesn't know I'm acting. If they knew that, I'd consider myself a failure."

Then he grinned and said: "But I really don't care what they mean, even if I don't understand it, because I know they aren't criticizing."

He once told another interviewer: "My goal is that the audience must never see the wheels go around, not see the work that goes into this. It must seem effortless and real. I don't do anything very consciously except that my end results must never be obvious in any way."

Fonda stayed with The Caine Mutiny Court Martial through May 1954, when he was offered the chance to recreate Mr. Roberts for the screen.

Jack Warner had bought the film rights to Mister Roberts, but he wanted a "younger" actor for the role of the executive officer. William Holden was considered. So was Marlon Brando, who accepted the offer.

But John Ford was hired to direct, and he wanted Fonda.

"Mr. Roberts is Fonda's part," Ford said. "He's right for it on the stage, and he's right for it on the screen. If he doesn't do this picture, then I don't do it, either."

The Ford-Fonda team was back. "I think I can say that after all our years together, we were a love story," Fonda said. "He loved me just like he loved Duke Wayne and Ward Bond."

Shooting started in September 1954 at locations on Midway Island and the Kaneohe Marine Corps Air Station at Honolulu. But trouble brewed in the Pacific paradise.

Henry Fonda, who after all these years had come to consider Mr. Roberts "his," had some fixed ideas about how it should come to the screen. He—and Leland Hayward—disliked many of the changes Ford was making. He had added a great deal of physical comedy in exteriors and enlarged some minor roles.

As Fonda recalled, "We had spent a lot of years to-

Ma'am, I sure like that name—Clementine.

As Wyatt Earp in *My Darling Clementine*

gether, and he was sensitive enough toward me to know that I was upset. One afternoon, he called me into his room. He was sitting in a wicker chair chewing on a handkerchief. Leland sat down on the bed. Pappy turned to me and said, 'Okay, what's the matter? I know something's eating you.'

"I said, 'Pappy, everybody knows you're the best director in the business. I wouldn't presume to tell you what to do, but I was in this play for seven years, and I have to be honest and say what I think. You're making some big mistakes.'

"Then I told him what they were. I don't know how far this conversation got, but suddenly he rose up out of the chair and threw a big haymaker and Pow!, hit me right in the jaw. It knocked me over backwards, and I crashed into some furniture.

"Well, that's about all there was to it. I was more embarrassed than hurt. I just walked out of the room. Half an hour later, Pappy came up to my room to apologize, not a big deal.

"But from then on, our relationship never was what it once had been."

Ford never did finish the picture. He was rushed to the hospital for emergency surgery and Mervyn LeRoy was called in to complete the shooting. Hayward did some extensive editing and recutting, with the result that *Mister Roberts*, with James Cagney as the phlegmatic captain, Jack Lemmon as Ensign Pulver, and William Powell, out of retirement to play Doc, became one of America's favorite movies. Lemmon won an Oscar for it.

Though he never publicly criticized it, Fonda was not among the movie's fans.

Interestingly, it was only the second time he had repeated a stage role he created for the screen. The other was his first film, *The Farmer Takes a Wife*. (His creations have been played on screen by others, however, including José Ferrer in *The Caine Mutiny*, and Walter Matthau in *First Monday in October*.)

The movie *Mister Roberts* also served to underscore Fonda's startling ability to alternate between stage and screen with no loss of performance perfection.

"I've switched back and forth so many times, I don't have any problem adjusting to the different requirements of the two media," he told AP's Bill Glover. "You do four bad pictures—knowing they'll probably be box office—hoping that they'll let you do one that is personally satisfying. The important thing is that you have to keep yourself in the producer's eye as well as in the public's so that you remain in demand.

"Sometimes you turn down something that turns out good. But I couldn't care less. The money difference between stage and screen isn't that important. And I don't look back."

There was no secret, however, that he preferred the stage.

"Having a live audience has nothing to do with it," he once said. "I can get just as much personal satisfaction in an empty house or before twenty people if I feel it's a good performance. But what is important is that in a play you can still be building a scene, improving it after three years. In the movies, there's never a chance to improve after that first morning, when the scene is shot and put in the can forever."

He later added this assessment: "In the theater, the actor does a complete job at each performance, inspired by the audience, whose response prevents his job from becoming tiresome. For in the theater, the audience is constantly changing, while in pictures the same director is the only audience and the sole judge of the performance.

"I prefer acting for a lot of different people rather than for one man."

Josh Logan saw his stage acting as a virtual religion.

Fonda has deep within him a small but inextinguishable flame that burns in worship of the art of the theater. He is one of the high priests of that art. When he feels laxness, insincerity, dilettantism around him, Hank can fly into short-lived tantrums and his votive flame can become a holocaust. . . .

Henry Fonda was also a father again, though not in the usual manner.

He and Susan had adopted an infant girl in 1954. They named her Amy.

"I don't like to say adoption," Fonda said in telling Howard Teichmann about her. "Because the baby we got is our daughter, no one else's daughter."

He added this telling remark: "I'd never had a chance to be a proper father to Jane or Peter when they were infants. . . . But now, with Amy, I used to be the one who got up at five o'clock in the morning. I gave her the bottles and I burped her. I just had a ball!"

At about the same time, Omaha provided an opportunity for Fonda to share a memorable experience with daughter Jane. The Omaha Community Playhouse, Fonda's crib stage, had asked him and Dorothy McGuire to return for a fund-raising performance of *The Country Girl*, the Clifford Odets play about an alcoholic actor and his wife. Both agreed to do it.

Then Henry's sister Harriet called to suggest an actress for the ingenue role.

"Why don't you bring out Jane?" she said.

"Have you lost your mind, Harriet? Forget it."

The Fonda family prepares to leave New York on a flight to Los Angeles in June 1954. From left to right are Fonda's third wife, Susan Blanchard, their infant daughter, Amy, Fonda, and his children, Jane and Peter.

At a rehearsal for *The Country Girl*, Henry and daughter Jane.

A rehearsal for *The Country Girl* at the Omaha Community Playhouse in 1955. From left are James Millhollin, playhouse director Kendrick Wilson, Jim Harker, Dorothy McGuire, Fonda, and daughter, Jane, in her stage debut.

In a formal scene from *War and Peace,*
from left are Fonda, Barry Jones, Hepburn,
and Mel Ferrer.

Overleaf: Henry Fonda and Audrey Hepburn relax on the set of *War and Peace,* filmed in Rome in 1955.

Opposite: Fonda and Susan (to his right) at a Paris fashion show, 1955. (*Inset*) On another trip, Susan is shown reviewing documents with a customs officer at Rome's Ciampino Airport in 1955 as Henry and Peter look on. The family had accompanied the actor to Europe, where he was filming the movie *War and Peace*.

During the filming of the movie of the famous clown's life in which he starred, Fonda watches as Emmet Kelly announces his engagement to Elvira Gebhardt in 1955.

PAA
PAA
PAA
PAA
New York Post Sports
Mays Expected Slump
-And He's in One Now

Nonetheless, Jane Fonda made her debut on the same stage her father did and that her brother was to appear on later. She was quite good, too.

After the Omaha performances, the whole Fonda family, Henry, Susan, Jane, Peter, and Amy, went to Rome where Fonda had signed on to play the role of Pierre in the Dino De Laurentiis production of War and Peace, with Audrey Hepburn and Mel Ferrer.

It was not a very satisfying trip for any of them.

Susan soon found, as Frances had, that Henry's most consuming love was his work. They drifted further and further apart.

In December of 1955, they parted after five years of marriage. Their announcement said his film commitments had "separated him from his wife for some time." The next May, they were divorced.

Susan received custody of Amy, then just over two years old. Property matters were settled in a private agreement that had been signed the previous January. "I was ashamed as hell," Fonda said later, "that a guy with a solid background like mine kept screwing up his personal life."

Work wasn't going well for Fonda, either. "Their idea of Pierre," said Fonda, "was that he look as much like Rock Hudson as possible." The result, critics harped, was that War and Peace was an overlong costume epic.

But it was during the filming of War and Peace—"it took longer to shoot than any picture I'd ever done"—that Henry Fonda met the willowy, effervescent Afdera Franchetti. Their relationship continued while Fonda was back in New York filming Alfred Hitchcock's Wrong Man.

On March 10, 1957, they were married in Fonda's Manhattan home on the posh Upper East Side. Peter, then a seventeen-year-old student at Westminster Academy in Simsbury, Connecticut, was his father's best man. Maria Stella Sernas, of Rome, a childhood friend of the bride's, was matron of honor. Jane, then a Vassar student, was also present. The bride was twenty-four, Fonda nearly fifty-two.

They postponed their wedding trip because Fonda was still filming Stage Struck, a remake of Morning Glory in which he played a worldly, sophisticated Broadway producer involved with a young actress (Susan Strasberg).

Fonda had formed his own producing company and started work on Clown, a picture that would recount the life of Emmett Kelly. But he put the project aside to make the movie version of the successful television drama 12 Angry Men. The film received good reviews but did disappointing business at the box office. Fonda, who had deferred his salary as producer-star, received no financial return for the effort.

The film, however, was nominated for a Best Picture Oscar and later won first prize at the Berlin Film Festival and at other international showings.

Fonda took the summer of 1958 to join Jane and Peter and Amy—he had Amy for July and August—along with his sister, Harriet, in Hyannisport on Cape Cod. While there, he was persuaded to perform in The Male Animal with Jane. "She really knocked me over," he said. "She was absolutely delightful, charming and natural." But he didn't tell her so.

Around this time, Fonda starred in two additional Hollywood Westerns, The Tin Star and Warlock, then made The Man Who Understood Women. He was on a second honeymoon in Europe when he agreed to return to Broadway in a play called Two for the Seesaw, about a Nebraska lawyer and his affair with a girl from the Bronx. Anne Bancroft played opposite him.

Then, lured by the promise of cash up front and future residuals, Henry Fonda turned to television. He had had offers before but turned them down, agreeing only to do some scenes from Mister Roberts for an "Ed Sullivan Show," a one-hour Arrowsmith, and a role in an adaptation of The Petrified Forest.

Now he decided to participate in a series called "The Deputy." In six of the thirty-nine episodes, he starred as the chief marshal of Arizona Territory in the 1880s; in the others, he appeared briefly as narrator and actor. The series, in addition to the lucrative financial arrangement, also scheduled his shooting during the summer and early fall, allowing him to star at the same time in Broadway's Silent Night, Lonely Night, the Robert Anderson play.

"They kept urging me to do a Western television series," he told an interviewer then, "and I kept resisting them. 'How different can you be with a Western?' I asked them. But they just laughed and said, 'Sit down, son, and let us tell you the facts of life. There are going to be more and more Westerns on television forever and ever.'"

His initial resistance to doing a Western television series was not based on a dislike of Westerns. He liked them—"if they're good, with believable characters and some humor and credible situations, instead of 'they went thataway' incidents." But he did not want to become type cast as a specific character. He often felt the public thought of him primarily as a movie Western hero even though Westerns made up only a small part of his credits.

He noted one other aspect: "I'm not much good on a horse. But I have to try to look good. I like to think it's not my fault. It's the fault of the horse.

"It looks so simple. There I am, and there's the horse at the hitching post, and there's the camera. But the instant I untie the horse and swing around to mount, the horse begins backing away. There he is with his tail in

Henry, Jane, and Peter are shown taking off from a New York airport for a summer vacation in Europe.

Fonda and the contessa pose for photographers at a Manhattan theater on March 7, 1957. (Fonda was in New York on location for the film *Stage Struck*.) Several days later, the two were married in a ceremony at Fonda's Upper East Side home. It was Fonda's fourth marriage, the first for the contessa, who was twenty-four years old. (*above left*). Actor Henry Fonda and his new bride, the former Italian Contessa Afdera Franchetti, are shown shortly after their wedding in New York City (*above right*). An early photo of Fonda with Contessa Afdera Franchetti of Italy on the set of *The Tin Star* at the Paramount studio in Hollywood in 1957 (*left*).

Opposite: Fonda and his wife walk arm in arm down Rome's fashionable Via Veneto during a private visit to Rome in May, 1960.

Fonda with his twenty-two year old daughter Jane.

Fonda with Francis Fuller, president of the American Academy of Dramatic Arts, at the premiere of the film *On the Beach* in New York City, 1959.

the cameraman's face, and I'm on the other side of him somewhere, and then the director yells disgustedly, 'Cut.'"

Once in the late 1930s, while playing in *The Virginian* at Westchester Playhouse in Mt. Kisco, a horse threw him, and he broke his wrist. "You wonder why I feel the way I do about horses?"

While filming new episodes of "The Deputy," Fonda also appeared on Broadway in *Critic's Choice*, in which he played a drama critic.

It's nearly thirteen hundred miles from Omaha to Broadway, more than sixteen hundred to Hollywood. As America entered its turbulent sixties and Henry Fonda bounded into his sixth decade, it was abundantly clear that he had conquered those twin hallmarks of his profession.

Surely, "exposure," to the public or to producers, was not a problem. He continued to alternate between stage and screen, perhaps with more consistent success than any other American actor, and offered his accomplished artistry more and more to the maturing medium of television. At the same time, his private life was bared to increasing media scrutiny as his children made news on their own.

On New Year's Day, 1960, Henry Fonda learned that Margaret Sullavan was dead, a suicide.

Early in 1961, Fonda put his fourth marriage behind him.

"I can only reproach myself," said the former Italian

baroness Afdera Franchetti. "Hank is an admirable man. I guess I was too immature."

The Juarez, Mexico, divorce court called it "incompatibility." Henry Fonda vowed he would never marry again.

He had finished his role on Broadway in *Critic's Choice*. During its run, Jane had made her movie debut in *Tall Story*, directed by Josh Logan.

On screen, Fonda appeared in *The Man Who Understood Women*, then *Advise and Consent*—the first in a threesome of political pictures in which he played a secretary of state, a presidential candidate (*The Best Man*), and finally, a president of the United States (on the "hot line" to Moscow in *Fail Safe*). Fonda personally wasn't much of a political activist, but he had teamed with John Steinbeck to support Adlai Stevenson (that characterization is obvious in *The Best Man*) and helped in the campaign of John F. Kennedy and, later, in that of John Tunney in California.

Upon finishing *Advise and Consent*, Fonda went to New York to see Peter make his Broadway debut in *Blood, Sweat and Stanley Poole* in which he played an Ivy League-type army draftee.

Fonda then played a bit role in the all-star *The Longest Day*, the story of D-day, portraying Gen. Theodore Roosevelt, Jr., and had a role in another all-star lineup for *How the West Was Won*, a Cinerama Western in which he was a grizzled buffalo hunter who befriends George Peppard—a friendship that existed off-screen as well.

He returned to Broadway in Garson Kanin's *Gift of*

Fonda and actor Allen Case relax on the set of "The Deputy," a 1959 television adventure Western series.

Time, with Olivia De Havilland. A play about a man who faces death from cancer, it didn't run long.

Then, through a press agent, he met a tall, slim airline stewardess, Shirlee Mae Adams, of Aurora, Illinois. She quickly became his constant date. He would take her to movie openings and made sure to get on her flights when traveling coast to coast while filming *Sex and the Single Girl*, another Western, *The Rounders*, and *In Harm's Way* (a cameo role as an admiral).

Years later, Fonda was asked whether he had ever appeared in any picture whose memory still made him shudder. "Sure," he said, "quite a few." The worst? "*Sex and the Single Girl*," he replied.

He took Shirlee with him to Spain in March 1965 when he filmed *The Battle of the Bulge*, and to the pre-Broadway tour of *Generation*.

Then the man who promised himself he'd never marry again proposed to Shirlee Adams, ex-airline hostess.

They were married December 3, 1965, in the chambers of State Supreme Court Justice Edwin B. Lynde in Mineola, New York. Actor George Peppard was best man and actress Elizabeth Ashley maid of honor. The only other witnesses were Fonda's long-time friend and publicity agent John Springer (who was later to write a book *The Fondas*) and Mrs. Springer.

Fonda was sixty; Shirlee thirty-three.

With a reference to his previous at-bats with brides, Fonda said, "I finally hit a home run."

It didn't happen right away, but friends and family noticed it. Fonda's restless spirit finally turned tranquil after his marriage to Shirlee. He told biographer

Henry Fonda attending a political demonstration for Adlai Stevenson at the Democratic National Convention in Los Angeles in July 1960.

Henry and Jane celebrate Father's Day in 1963. Fonda paid a surprise visit to his daughter while she was at work in Hollywood on the M-G-M movie *Sunday in New York.*

Fonda takes a break on the set of *Sex and the Single Girl.*

Henry escorts Shirlee Adams, an airline hostess, to the Hollywood premiere of the film *It's A Mad, Mad, Mad, Mad World* in 1963 (*top*). During rehearsals for *Sex and the Single Girl* in 1964 with costars Barbara Bouchet, left, and Lauren Bacall (*bottom*).

Opposite: Henry Fonda, 1964. (*Inset*) A year later, on December 3, 1965, Fonda, sixty, married the thirty-three-year-old Shirlee.

Teichmann, "Shirlee turned me around. I'm easier with her than I've been with anyone before. Maybe I'm mellowing with age. Maybe with Shirlee I'm more willing to compromise."

The wedding took place two months after the Broadway opening of *Generation*, an amiable comedy about an advertising executive and his kooky son-in-law that involved the confusions between elders and youngsters as well as the basic facts of procreation.

Fonda once referred to that role of the confused father, noting, "I was a living authority on the subject."

The Fonda patriarch never denied his shortcomings as a father. He noted in retrospect that he was away a great deal when his children were growing up, fighting in World War II during some of their key growing-up years and often away on location filming or show touring. When he was at home, he found it virtually impossible to express love for his children.

In the sixties, when a national generation gap focused on the Vietnam War and drug and motorcycle cults, the Fondas could have served as prime symbols. Jane, particularly, had generated wide controversy for her advocacy of liberal and radical causes, and Peter, especially through his film *Easy Rider*, became identified with those cults.

Fonda told an interviewer that being a movie star kept him from being a good father to his children, who became what they were in spite of him. "I didn't help or discourage them or lead them by the hand," he said. "I'm not trying to set myself up as a good father. But I think I knew instinctively that if they did make it, they would like to know they did it on their own."

"Peter and Jane were successful very young," he said at another time. "Their rebellions against me as a parent didn't last too long. They willingly admitted, 'I'm sorry, dad, for the hurtful things that were said.' Jane said plenty of hurtful things to the press. She told one reporter she grew up in a completely phony atmosphere."

"Sure, I might have done things differently with my children if I had another chance. But I'm not sure anything would have changed. Why, I never even told my children 'I love you' until Peter forced it out of me."

Peter did "force" it out of him, however, and their relationship, the whole family relationship, did come together in later years.

Jane Fonda visits her father backstage at Broadway's Morosco Theatre in 1966 while he was starring in the hit play *Generation* (*top*). At another performance, Fonda is greeted after the show by, from left, Robert Preston, Van Johnson, Mia Farrow, and Rosalind Russell (*bottom*).

45

I'll be all around in the dark—I'll be everywhere. Wherever you can look—wherever there's a fight, so hungry people can eat, I'll be there. Wherever there's a cop beating up a guy—I'll be there. I'll be there in the way guys yell when they're mad. I'll be there in the way kids laugh when they're hungry, and they know supper's ready, and when people are eatin' the stuff they raised, and livin' in the houses they built—I'll be there, too.

As Tom Joad in *The Grapes of Wrath*

Henry played a role in *Wanda Nevada*, which Peter produced and directed. And, finally, he and Jane blended talents, playing father and daughter in the emotionally stirring *On Golden Pond*. In a scene in that deservedly award-winning film, in a rowboat in the middle of the pond, the two try to overcome the emotional distance between them.

"We've been mad at each other for so long . . ." she says.

"I didn't know we were mad at each other," he answers. "I thought we just didn't like each other."

Jane was to recall later: "I reached out to take his arm, and I felt him shudder, because he wasn't expecting it. He's not an emotional actor, and everyone on the crew saw it. I took his arm and said. 'I want to be your friend,' and I felt him trying to keep the tears back. It was a moment of such intimacy. . . ."

When Fonda received the Life Achievement Award from the American Film Institute, the whole Fonda flock was there. Fonda, with pride and emotion, pointed them out from the stage:

"That's Shirlee—with two Es—in the middle. Every good thing that happens to me is always twice as good because I get to share it with her. Like tonight.

"On Shirlee's right is my son—the hyphenate. Peter is the original hyphenate. When he was twelve years old in a boarding school, he organized a theater group—wrote the play, directed it, and played three parts. Can you wonder that I'm in awe of him?

"On his right is his Bridget . . . Next to her, Justin—one of the great hitters in the Little League. Next to Justin is Peter's wife, a Montana rancher, Portia.

"On the other side of Shirlee is Jane's family. . . . Tom had to take Troy, the youngster, to bed just about five minutes ago, he's missing this. But I want to say that Tom Hayden, who's Jane's husband, makes me think of a lot of the parts that I played, you know, the mavericks and dissenters—except he ain't play-acting. And that little one next to the empty chair is my Vanessa—the girl scout dropout.

"And then, there's my youngest daughter, Amy,

who's down from Colorado where she's preparing for her masters in social work. Does that make her the white sheep of the family?"

Then he added: "In the years since my dad's left us, I've done some things I know that he wouldn't have approved. I hope that I've done some things that he would've defended.

"I know he'd bust his buttons tonight. He never met my children, but I know he'd be proud. I can hear dad answering somebody criticizing Jane . . .

"'Shut up, she's perfect!' Right on, dad!"

Fonda also delved into television, first carefully, with brief appearances, then for specials, finally for two series. The significant specials included readings from excerpts of John Steinbeck's *America and the Americans,* that prize-winning author's love song to his country and his countrymen. Later, he was to appear in television adaptations of Steinbeck's *Travels With Charley* and *The Red Pony*.

When Steinbeck died in December 1968, Fonda lost a great and dear friend. He flew off to New York to read three short poems, by Synge, Tennyson, and Robert Louis Stevenson, at the memorial service.

After the service, he returned to Steinbeck's home with the author's widow, Elaine. She gave him a silver box. It was an old tobacco can, decorated by Steinbeck. Inside were the pearl studs he had worn when he won the Nobel Prize for Literature. "He wanted you to have this," his widow said.

In 1968, after a friendship then thirty-six years strong, Henry Fonda finally got around to appearing in a film with Jimmy Stewart.

It was *Firecreek*. Fonda played the baddie, a gang leader; Stewart, the timid sheriff. They were to team again one more time, in 1970, in *The Cheyenne Social Club*, another Western. In this one, Stewart inherits a bordello.

Firecreek wasn't the only time Fonda was the villain. Not even close.

Henry, Jane, and Peter in 1976. It was the first time that Fonda had posed with them together in more than ten years.

Fonda, wearing a beard for a movie role, appears in superior court in Los Angeles, December 2, 1966, to give "moral support" to his son Peter, on trial for possession of marijuana.

Father and daughter, actor and actress, as they appear together on the "Today Show" in Los Angeles, May 1979.

Sergio Leone, Italy's famed and profitable director of "spaghetti Westerns," cast Fonda as the heavy in *Once Upon a Time in the West.* It was difficult for American audiences to take Henry Fonda murdering a man and his three children in cold blood before the picture really got started.

Early in the 1970s, Fonda tried again to make a success of a television series. After his unhappy experience with "The Deputy," he tried "The Smith Family," in which he played a devoted family man, a police officer, and father of three. It was disappointing, too.

He also was one of the first major stars to make a deal to do commercials, most notably those for GAF.

"The commercials were better than some movies I've made," he said, "so why dodge them? People liked them, and in my business the operative word is 'exposure.' Good exposure is always good whether it is on Broadway, on television, or even appearing on behalf of a candidate. . . ."

At the same time, he was touring the country on stage. In 1972, he did *The Time of Your Life,* which was on a fifteen-week tour, at the John F. Kennedy Center in Washington. In it, he played Joe, the champagne-drinking man from William Saroyan's Pulitzer Prize-winning play, opposite Jane Alexander. The AP's Donald Sanders said Fonda gave his usual superb performance, giving imperious commands to his errand boy, bringing his great technical skill to Saroyan's poetic lines, and singing a hilarious "Let the Lower Lights Be Burning" with Strother Martin. The highlight of the evening was a gum-chewing contest between Fonda and Martin in which Fonda chewed thirty-two sticks of gum and still managed to make himself understandable.

Meanwhile, he had appeared on screen in *Yours, Mine and Ours* with Lucille Ball, *Madigan* with Richard Widmark, *The Boston Strangler*, *There Was a Crooked Man*, and *Too Late the Hero*.

In 1974, he accepted the title role in the one-man stage drama *Clarence Darrow.* He liked it so much that he turned down the opportunity to play another "beautiful piece of work." *Darrow*, he thought, was a "once-in-a-lifetime thing." The play, by David Rintels, chronicles the life of the noted attorney who surged through the law courts like a one-man American Civil Liberties Union for half a century.

With no makeup except some stomach padding and an artificial forelock, Fonda soloed in an incredibly evocative portrait. He recreated the role for television later in the year, giving that mass and often mediocre medium one of its finest moments.

Meanwhile, he continued work in the movies. There was *Sometimes a Great Notion; Ash Wednesday; The Serpent; My Name is Nobody; Midway* (he played Admiral Nimitz); *Rollercoaster* (a bit role); *The Swarm* (an all-star disaster); *Meteor* (another role as president of the United States); and *Fedora* (as himself).

In April 1980, he appeared twice on network television. One harked back to television's beginnings. In a live drama, *The Oldest Living Graduate,* he played Col. J. C. Kincaid, the invalided but still lively patriarch of a west Texas family and oldest living graduate of a military academy. It was produced by David Rintels, author of *Clarence Darrow.*

"Live television doesn't bother me," Fonda said at the time. "This is the way we did it all the time eighteen-twenty years ago. I never had any mishaps during a show. Even when they do happen, I don't think the audience realizes it. Only the actors are aware."

"I was in the first live program broadcast from the NBC studios from Burbank—did *Petrified Forest* with Humphrey Bogart and Lauren Bacall [in 1955]. She was scared to death because she hadn't appeared in much theater; but after the first few minutes into the show, she was terrific. As for Bogie, no problem. He was playing a role [Duke Mantee] he had created."

Fonda played Colonel Kincaid with a decided southern accent—not a first time for him. "I've done it in *The*

I want to call for a vote. I want you eleven men to vote by secret ballot. I'll abstain. If there are still eleven votes for guilty, I won't stand alone. We'll take in a guilty verdict right now.

As Juror 8 in *12 Angry Men*

Henry Fonda narrating a 1967 network television
special based on John Steinbeck's *America and Americans*. Fonda had been a great fan of Steinbeck's for
many years, even prior to his role as Tom Joad in *The
Grapes of Wrath*.

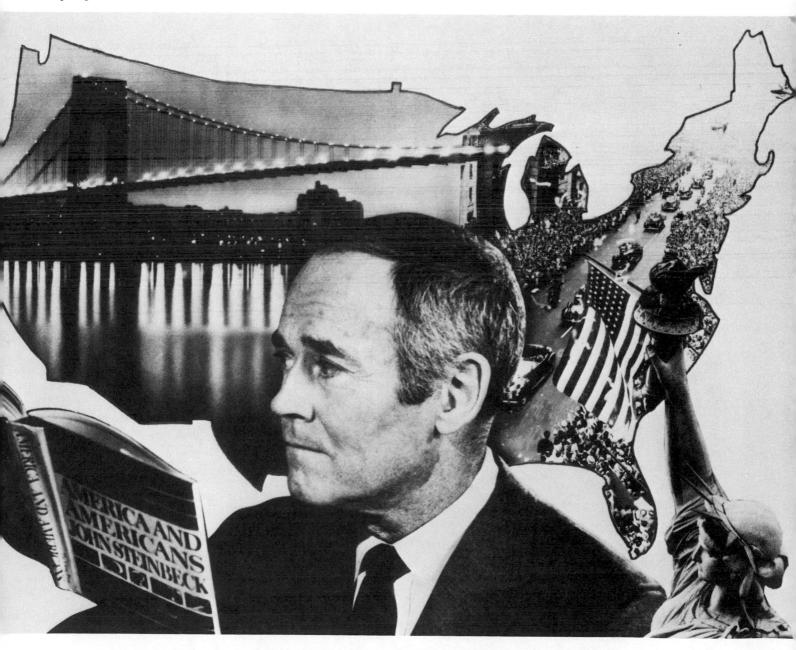

Fonda and his wife, Shirlee, arrive for the opening of *The Lion in Winter* at the Lincoln Arts Theatre in New York, October 1968. The movie starred Katharine Hepburn, later to be Fonda's last costar in a major motion picture (*top*). Fonda and Shirlee out on the town, this time at the Los Angeles Music Center for a television and movie industries gala in June 1971 (*bottom*).

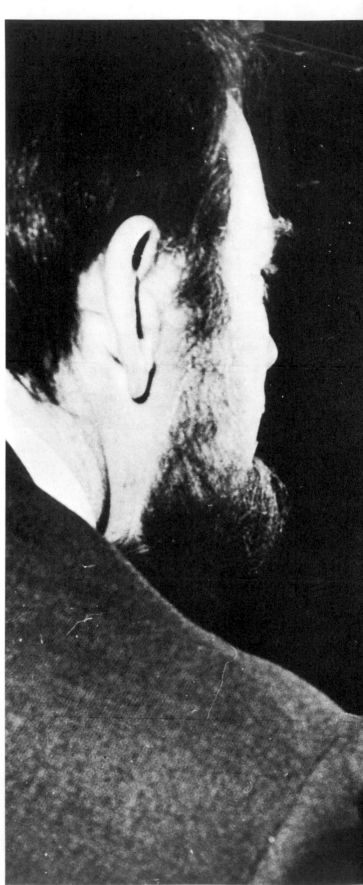

Henry Fonda prepares for his stage role in *The Trial of Abraham Lincoln* at the Los Angeles Huntington Hartford Theater in April 1971.

Fonda stars with Joanne Woodward and Gerald Michenaud in the 1973 made-for-television movie "A Big Hand for the Little Lady."

During the 1970s, Fonda appeared in a number of other television series and specials. Here he is shown with the cast of "The Smith Family." They are, from left to right, Darlene Carr, Janet Blair, Michael James Wixted, Fonda, and Ronald Howard.

Fonda takes a chance at the presidency himself when he runs as a candidate on the television series "Maude," also in 1975.

Here he appears the same year in a scene from the ninety-minute television version of *Clarence Darrow*, based on the life of the famous lawyer.

Fonda is joined by his family following a performance of his one-man show *Clarence Darrow* at the Huntington Hartford Theater in Los Angeles in June 1974. Fonda, who was sixty-nine years old, had recently undergone surgery for implantation of a heart pacemaker. From left to right, surrounding Fonda, are Jane, Shirlee, Peter, and Amy.

Henry Fonda appears as Gen. Douglas MacArthur in the 1975 television special "Collision Course" (*right*). In that same production, E. G. Marshall plays the role of President Harry Truman (*left*).

Opposite: Henry Fonda as an aging Illinois farmer who has a strong ally in his young granddaughter, played by Kristen Vigard, in the drama "Home to Stay," another of Henry's television movies, aired in 1978.

Henry Fonda, as himself, 1976.

Fonda appears with actresses Shirley MacLaine, left, and Liza Minelli as hosts of a three-hour television special entitled "Life Goes to the Movies," which was presented in 1976.

NEW RADIANCE FOR AMERICAN CHURCHES
THE MODERN RENAISSANCE OF STAINED-GLASS ART

LIFE

A GARDEN OF SHRUBS TO PLANT NOW

Opposite: Fonda in the very successful television production "Roots II: The Next Generation," which ran in 1979. (*Inset*) Fonda portrays a gun fighter past his prime in the Western satire "My Name is Nobody," shown on television in 1978.

Fonda demonstrates his acting skills to Quinn Cummings, left, and director Joanne Woodward on the set of the television series "Family" in an episode that premiered in November 1979.

Cheyenne Social Club, Roots, and, oh, a half-dozen other southern roles, but never as broad as this," he said.

The other television special that month was "Gideon's Trumpet," filmed at the California Men's Prison at Chino, again reuniting Rintels with Fonda. It is the story of Clarence Earl Gideon, a criminal whose handwritten appeal to the U.S. Supreme Court in 1962 resulted in the overturning of his sentence, a new trial, and eventual acquittal.

Again, Fonda played the people's defender. He himself said Gideon could have been Tom Joad grown up.

Henry Fonda's last appearance on Broadway was in 1978, costarring with Jane Alexander, then Eva Marie Saint, in *First Monday in October*, portraying Supreme Court Justice Daniel Snow in the story of the first woman

Supreme Court justice. (The film version costarred Walter Matthau and Jill Clayburgh.)

It wasn't all work, however. When not on stage, Fonda had his painting, his gardening, and his beekeeping. The painting really began while he was appearing in *Mister Roberts* on Broadway. It was then kind of an extension of the set and scenery painting that kept him working during those early acting years.

He developed into a skilled painter, though chiefly of still lifes, starting with pastels, then going on to oils, water-color, even working with clay. He was also adept at needlepoint. Some of his canvasses adorned his home; many were given to friends and colleagues.

During the filming of *The Cheyenne Social Club*, Fonda sketched a picture of Jimmy Stewart's horse, Pie. Stewart, unlike his friend, loved horses and had been riding Pie in movies for twenty years. Fonda drew the

Opposite: at the age of seventy-four, Henry Fonda appears in a live television broadcast of the play *The Oldest Living Graduate*, which was broadcast from Southern Methodist University in Dallas, Texas, on April 7, 1980. Fonda stars as the oldest and saltiest living graduate of a Texas military academy.

Fonda and actor-producer John Houseman during a break in the filming of *Gideon's Trumpet*, at the California Men's Institution at Chino, in 1979.

Actress Sylvia Sidney is another backstage visitor during Fonda's run in *First Monday in October*. In the background is a poster from the 1935 film *Trail of the Lonesome Pine*, in which the two appeared.

Fonda holds the arm of a friend and fellow actor James Stewart as he greets visitors following his performance in the play *First Monday in October*, in October 1978. Costar Jane Alexander stands behind Fonda.

Henry Fonda, at far left, is among those gathered in December 1978 for a public reading of the United States Constitution. The reading, which took place at New York's Broadway Theatre, was a project of the William O. Douglas Inquiry, a foundation named for Douglas, a U.S. Supreme Court justice. Others shown in the picture are, from left to right, Melvyn Douglas, Myrna Loy, Anne Jackson, Eli Wallach, former Rep. Helen Gahagan Douglas, and former Supreme Court Justice Abe Fortas.

Fonda is backstage again, this time with his wife, Shirlee, to congratulate Phyllis Newman following a performance in New York in 1979.

Fonda and Rock Hudson, left, appear backstage at the Palace Theatre in New York in 1979 to give a boost to fellow actor Joel Grey, who was starring in the musical Grand Tour (*below left*). That same year, also in New York, he gives an affectionate hug to actress Imogene Coca during a party to celebrate her fiftieth anniversary in show business (*below right*).

Fonda shown concentrating on his needlepoint, a favorite hobby, in 1977.

Fonda, an avid beekeeper, checks on the hives behind his Bel-Air home in June 1980.

Middle age means the middle, Ethel. The middle of life. People don't live to be 150 . . . You're old and I'm ancient.

As Norman Thayer in *On Golden Pond*

horse, the barn, a carriage, and the gate, finished the water-color at home, and surprised Stewart with a framed painting. It meant a great deal to his friend.

Fonda, who was considered the most talented of all the celebrities with that hobby, preferred to present his paintings as gifts, but he did sell one at auction once, for $23,000.

He also once participated in a show business art show called "Visual Arts by Performing Artists." An art critic noted that Fonda "goes in for the fool-the-eye realism in the manner of Hartnett." His painting in the show was an "interior," consisting of a lantern, rope, and chain against a crude wooden wall.

Fonda, the "squire of Chalon Road," was equally proud of his farming and beekeeping. Beekeeping was one of the reasons he tried late in his life not to be away from his Bel-Air estate more than twelve weeks at a time. "Also, it's not fair to my family to be away any longer," he said. "And besides the bees, I have five dogs and chickens, my garden and fruit trees."

He tried to arrange his filming locations to be close enough to attend his crops. One year he planned to make cider from his five apple trees, noting, "I was always told that you couldn't grow apples in this climate. About forty years ago, I went to the nursery and asked if they had an apple tree that would grow here. Yes, they did, and it was called Beverly Hills. I planted some at my old house on Tigertail, and they did great. They burned in the Bel-Air fire along with the house; I had since sold it.

"I planted more when I moved into this house. I've used the fruit for apple sauce, apple pies, apple butter. This year I'm going to try cider, honest-to-goodness hard cider."

He also enjoyed passing out jars of honey to his theatrical colleagues and always had a jar ready for the knowing hostess who invited him and Shirlee to dinner.

"We've noted an upswing in our dinner invitations," he joked. "I really have a tough time keeping up with the demand."

Despite those interests, he kept up a heady pace of films, television movies, shows, specials, and, of course, the stage. As a septuagenarian, he was asked why. The fear of "never being asked to work again, no

one wanting me," he reasoned. "Sounds ridiculous, but that's why I sometimes take jobs I probably should pass by."

Any question of retirement got an emphatic "no, no, no" in reply.

"Why do that when it's still so much fun," he told AP's Bill Glover in 1978. "I don't mean that in a superficial way but as something thoroughly satisfying and deeply gratifying. I have to remind myself that I'm seventy-three years old, because I don't look it and I don't feel it.

"The big thing is joy in your work."

All that could slow him down—but only slow him down—was illness.

He collapsed after a performance of *Clarence Darrow* in 1974, was hospitalized, and had a pacemaker implanted in his chest to correct a heart-rhythm disorder. It kept him away only five weeks.

Two years later, he underwent an operation to remove a tumor on his diaphragm. In 1979, during the run of *First Monday in October*, he had minor hip and prostate surgery. He had further diagnostic heart surgery in 1981, later suffering a relapse of his heart ailment.

Perhaps prodded by these intimations of mortality, his professional colleagues began paying him long-due honors and tributes. He received the American Film Institute's prestigious Life Achievement Award, honoring his work, in 1978. The following year, he was one of five American artists receiving the second annual Kennedy Center honors. The five—Fonda, composer Aaron Copeland, singer Ella Fitzgerald, dancer-choreographer Martha Graham, and playwright Tennessee Williams—were introduced at a glittering White House reception, then proceeded to a sold-out gala attended by more than two thousand dignitaries in the Kennedy Center Opera House. There they watched scenes from *My Darling Clementine*, then *The Grapes of Wrath*, and *The Ox-Bow Incident*.

But the big surprise was yet to come. The curtain parted for ninety midshipmen from the U.S. Naval Academy Glee Club who sang "Anchors Aweigh," then "Red River Valley"—the theme song of *The Grapes of Wrath*.

After the vocalizing, a midshipman walked up to the microphone and said to Fonda: "Thank you, Mister

Italian director Franco Zeffirelli presents Fonda with an award for his lifelong contribution to film during the closing ceremonies of the International Movie Festival in Taormina, Sicily, July 1973.

The American Film Institute presents Henry Fonda with its Annual Award for Life Achievement in Motion Pictures and Television at ceremonies held in Beverly Hills on March 1, 1978 (*right*). His children, Jane and Peter, celebrate the honor with him (*far right*).

Roberts." Finally, each member of the glee club, as he left the stage, saluted and repeated "Thank you, Mister Roberts."

In January 1981, Fonda was honored by his acting alma mater, the Omaha Community Playhouse. Dorothy McGuire was there, as were Josh Logan and Peter and grandson Justin, then fourteen. Fonda called the boy up to the stage so he could say he was on the same stage as his grandfather, his father, and his aunt.

Fonda, who had often said, "We Fondas will cry at a good steak," was teary-eyed as he accepted the ovation. During a question-and-answer session, Fonda said he and his children, after some troubled times, had achieved close, loving relationships.

A voice in the audience proclaimed loudly: "Hear! Hear!" It was Peter.

Dorothy McGuire spoke. "We all know that he's the absolute top in theater. His artistry is that great. . . . But above and beyond that, he has shown us—actors—how to live. His energy extends in many directions: his generosity, his kindness, his standing for something, his interest in not only theater and causes but bees and butterflies and flowers and cooking—you name it."

In 1981, he also accepted an honorary Academy Award, "in recognition of his brilliant accomplishments and enduring contribution to the art of motion pictures."

Walking with a cane but holding his head high, Fonda said: "When I realize that I've been working in films for forty-six years, I feel I'm a very, very lucky man.

"Not just because I survived but because over the years I have had the opportunity to work with some of the best producers, the best directors, the best actors in motion pictures.

"It's been a very rewarding forty-six years for me. And this has got to be the climax."

Fonda honored with yet another well-deserved tribute, the Cecil B. De Mille Award, at the Hollywood Foreign Press Association's 1980 Golden Globe Awards in Los Angeles. The award was given for outstanding contributions to the entertainment industry. (*Top inset*) Actress Jane Fonda presents her father, Henry, with a special Tony Award for his achievement in drama during ceremonies in New York in June 1979. The special award was a surprise to the famous stage and screen actor. (*Bottom inset*) In January 1981, Fonda returned to his home in Omaha, Nebraska, as the Omaha Community Playhouse paid tribute to its most famous graduate. Fonda's wife, Shirlee, sits beside her husband. Standing behind them are Fonda's son, Peter, and his sister, Harriet Warren, a resident of Omaha (photo by Jim Burnett; used with kind permission of the *Omaha World Herald* and the photographer).

The tributes flowed like vintage wine; they were numerous, heartfelt, glowing. And the best was yet to come.

Ernest Thompson had written a play called *On Golden Pond*. It was about an elderly couple, Norman and Ethel Thayer, putting their lives in order because they knew death was not far away. They return to Golden Pond because it was special in their lives.

"Hepburn wanted to do Ethel," Thompson recalled, "but said nothing about who should play Norman. Henry wanted to play Norman but said nothing about Ethel. It was Jane who worked it all out. She's a very orderly, persuasive lady. She told me she was determined to do a picture with her father and that it was an absolute natural for Hepburn to be Ethel."

On that location site in Squam Lake, New Hampshire, that summer of 1980, Henry Fonda looked back on his life.

"Think of how lucky I've been these last few years," he told writer Richard Coe.

"At a time of life when there aren't many leading parts for an old duffer like me, I've had four beauts—Clarence Darrow in the one-man *Darrow*, Justice Dan Snow in *First Monday in October*, Colonel Kincaid in *The Oldest Living Graduate*. And here's Norman Thayer. Beautiful parts, all of them.

"Did you know I might have done George in Albee's *Who's Afraid of Virginia Woolf*? But the agent never sent it to me. I hit the roof and asked Albee to send me, personally, his next one. He did—*Seascape*—and I phoned him after reading it that I'd love to do it. In the same mail was another script, *Darrow*. I read it after phoning Albee. What a situation! I had to call Albee back to renege. Awful thing to do. But I couldn't have missed *Darrow*.

"This amounts to a family party. Shirlee and I have been married eighteen years, longest of my talked-about marriages. She's my real keeper. Nobody gets to me except through her. I'm the beekeeper, the only one in Bel-Air, I expect. I enjoy farming at our place. Must be the most expensive darned farming land in the whole earth. Think of that, me from Nebraska, Bel-Air farmer. . . .

"Do you realize Jane's won two Oscars—*Coming Home* and *Klute*—and I've never won one?"

On the first day of shooting, Katharine Hepburn gave Fonda a most special gift. It was Spencer Tracy's favorite hat.

Fonda promised to do a painting for her. He did it at home in Bel-Air. It was a painting of three hats: Spencer Tracy's battered felt hat, Fonda's rain hat, and his fishing hat.

After *On Golden Pond*, Fonda did a television movie with Myrna Loy, *Summer Solstice*, filmed on Cape Cod. "There I was," Fonda said, "back on Cape Cod where I started. Life is strange. It's like a big circle."

On Golden Pond opened in December 1981 and captured the hearts of moviegoers everywhere.

Opposite: In 1981, he is a special guest of honor at the Los Angeles Drama Critics Circle Awards Dinner.

Myrna Loy and Henry Fonda in a scene from the television production "Summer Solstice," which aired in 1981 (*right*). Fonda dining at a New York restaurant with Myrna Loy, center, and his wife, Shirlee, (*below*).

Henry with his first Oscar for Best Actor in *On Golden Pond*, presented by the Academy of Motion Pictures Arts and Sciences in March 1982. The Academy Award was accepted by his daughter, Jane, as he was too ill to attend the ceremonies. At his right is Fonda's wife, Shirlee.

Veteran actor James Stewart talks to the press before entering the home of his late friend Henry Fonda, who had died earlier that day, August 12, 1982.

Shirlee Fonda, second from right, widow of Henry Fonda, gathers with his children, Jane, Amy, and Peter (left to right), hours after the great actor's death in a Los Angeles hospital at age seventy-seven.

Oh, God, make me a good movie actor! Make me one of the best. For Jesus' sake, Amen.

As Merton In *Merton of the Movies*

Vincent Canby, movie critic of the *New York Times*, summed up the sentiment:

As Norman Thayer Jr., celebrating his eightieth birthday with reluctance, furiously aware of his physical and mental decline and as frightened of death as he is angry with it, Mr. Fonda gives one of the great performances of his long, truly distinguished career. Here is film acting of the highest order, the kind that is not discovered overnight in the laboratory, but seems to be the distillation of hundreds of performances.

As you watch him in *On Golden Pond*, you're seeing the intelligence, force and grace of a talent that has been maturing on the screen for almost fifty years, in everything from *You Only Live Once*, *Jesse James*, *The Grapes of Wrath*, *The Lady Eve* and *My Darling Clementine*, through *Mr. Roberts*, *12 Angry Men* and all of those more recent films in which he has given class to junk simply by his appearance in a cameo role.

In January 1982, Henry Fonda won the Foreign Press Association Golden Globe Award for the role. Unable to attend the ceremonies himself, Jane accepted it for him, saying: "My dad doesn't believe in these things but I'm still happy for him." She added that the role was "the highlight of Henry's life and his career."

Then, on the night of March 30, at the 54th Academy Awards, Henry Fonda was acclaimed Best Actor—his first and only Oscar.

"Father didn't think he would win," Jane Fonda said in accepting the award for him. "I know that he is very, very honored and very happy and very surprised. And I know he is saying, 'Hey, ain't I lucky!'—as though luck had anything to do with it."

Shirlee reported that Fonda had watched the ceremony on television. "He just burst into tears," she said. "He's so emotional."

Henry Jaynes Fonda died August 12, 1982.

According to his will, his widow Shirlee and his adopted daughter Amy were to share his estate. The decision to leave Jane and Peter out, the document said, "is not in any sense a measure of my deep affection for them" but because they were not dependent on him for their support.

The family suggested contributions be made to the Henry Fonda Memorial Theater, an addition to his beloved Omaha Community Playhouse.

His will noted that he wanted no service, no memorials. But there will always be memorials to Henry Fonda, in every showing of his films and in the hearts and memories of all those who saw and heard him perform.

Like Tom Joad, "He'll be all around in the dark."

ON THE BROADWAY STAGE

In January 1981, Henry Fonda pays his last visit to the Omaha Community
Playhouse—the stage on which he first performed (copyright Omaha
Community Playhouse; photo used with their kind permission).

"Now that Mr. Fonda is back after 11 years, it would be nice to have him back for good," suggested Brooks Atkinson, the distinguished *New York Times* critic on Henry Fonda's triumphant return to Broadway in 1948 in the lusty, yet bittersweet World War II navy comedy, *Mister Roberts*.

Fonda, forty years later said of his love of theater: "For me, the stage is like going on a holiday. In film and TV, you do the best you can, but the theater is where you really get a chance to act."

The tall, lanky Nebraskan with the prairie-flat accent never fulfilled Atkinson's wish "to have him back for good." Hollywood continued to have him for a career that encompassed films, television specials, and two television series, "The Deputy" and "The Smith Family." But Fonda's commitment to the stage never wavered. He always managed to take that "holiday," always returned to theaters, regional and in New York, appearing in seventeen Broadway plays in his lifetime.

He made his Broadway debut in 1929 as a walk-on in *A Game of Life and Death*. His last trip there, in 1978, was as a Supreme Court justice in *First Monday in October*.

Regional theater is where he first acted, though, and he never forgot his roots. The last acting he did was at the Hartman Theater Company in Stamford, Connecticut, in February 1981. He was seventy-six, ailing, and had to use a cane. It didn't matter. He still got raves. As Douglas Watt, drama critic of the New York *Daily News,* wrote at the time:

Seeing Henry Fonda in Lanny Flaherty's *Showdown at the Adobe Motel* is comparable to hearing Horowitz in person run through a book of Czerny etudes. The virtuosity is compelling even while the material is negligible.

Like many top actors before and after him, Fonda first made his reputation on the New York stage. The first break, in 1934, was in Leonard Sillman's first *New Faces*, in which Fonda showed his comic flair in sketches with another young unknown, Imogene Coca.

A year later, he achieved stardom as a virtuous farm boy in love with the daughter of river-boat folk in the comedy *The Farmer Takes a Wife*. Critic Atkinson, after seeing him in it, noted approvingly: "Henry Fonda, who has his first big opportunity here, gives a manly, modest performance in a style of captivating simplicity."

Simplicity. No wasted motion, an on-stage ease and naturalness that seemed real, without effort. This was the Fonda trademark, recognized early on by Broadway's Josh Logan, his director in *Mister Roberts* and a lifelong friend. The year was 1928, the place the Cape Playhouse in Cape Cod, Massachusetts. Fonda, a handsome, gangling newcomer to the University Players, played a brainless young boxer in *Is Zat So*. A forgettable play but a memorable performance. "Fonda wiped all of us off the stage simply by seeming to do nothing," Logan writes in *Josh*, his autobiography. "His understatement has become one of our national treasures."

Meticulous about his work but modest about his abilities, Fonda once described his approach to acting this way: "My goal is that the audience must never see the wheels go around, not see the work that goes into this."

The complex, laconic midwesterner never formally studied his craft. He learned by watching, listening, and doing. Still, in 1974, the acclaimed old pro was insisting: "I don't know anything about acting. I did it quite by accident; came out of the community theater after two or three years and then found you get paid for it in New York."

His accident occurred forty-nine years earlier back home in Nebraska, courtesy of Dorothy "Do" Brando, whose son, Marlon, was nominated for a Tony award in 1948—but lost to Fonda, star of *Mister Roberts*.

Mrs. Brando, a family friend, was active in the Omaha Community Theater. The troupe was starting its new season with Philip Barry's *You and I* and needed a juvenile. She called Fonda's mother. Young Henry was sent over and got the role. Inexperienced, insecure, he

Fonda and Dorothy McGuire in *The Country Girl* at the
Omaha Community Playhouse, 1955 (copyright
Omaha Community Playhouse; photo used with their
kind permission).

nonetheless was fascinated by theater life, which became his life on his first opening night.

The next season, he essayed his first starring role at the theater in *Merton of the Movies*, quit his $30-a-week clerk's job at the Retail Credit Company of Omaha, then went to make his way in the world.

The first paying job: playing the military secretary of Abraham Lincoln, the Great Emancipator played by George Billings, an ex-carpenter from Hollywood with a fondness for strong drink. They toured Nebraska, Iowa, Kansas. A hard life, but the road never fazed Fonda. Even in 1951, his stardom long since assured, he jumped at the chance to take live theater to America. Fonda toured in *Mister Roberts*, again playing the wry, idealistic navy lieutenant—the role on which he put his most distinctive stamp—for nine months after 1,157 performances on Broadway.

Not only did he enjoy trouping, he liked taking a good play with a good company out into the regional areas. "In Boston or Philadelphia or Chicago, they get first-class theater a lot," he said. "But to play Detroit, Pittsburgh, Kansas City, St. Louis, Portland, and Seattle, when you took 'em something they loved, they wanted to hug you and say thank you. They didn't get it often enough. That's a great feeling."

If there wasn't a tour and he had the time, he'd regularly pop in at regional theaters as a "guest star"—as in 1955, when he returned to his acting alma mater, the Omaha Community Theater, in *The Country Girl* in which daughter Jane made her stage debut.

In the early seventies, you'd find him at Long Island's Plumstead Playhouse, having the time of his life in revivals of *The Time of Your Life*, *Our Town*, and *The Front Page*.

But Broadway—which sent him to Hollywood and stardom in 1935, in the film version of *The Farmer Takes a Wife*—always is the main event for an actor, and Fonda was no exception. He kept coming back, usually with success, occasionally not—as in 1937, in a cliché-ridden romantic comedy, *Blow Ye Winds*, which blew town after thirty-six performances.

Between 1947 and 1958, he had four straight Broadway hits: *Mister Roberts*; *Point of No Return*, based on John P. Marquand's novel about an unhappy Manhattan banker from a small town; *The Caine Mutiny Court Martial*; and *Two for the Seesaw*, William Gibson's comedy about a conventional midwestern lawyer and an unconventional New York girl.

In 1960, Broadway had two Fondas: Henry in a modest success called *Critic's Choice*, and daughter Jane, in her New York debut in *There Was a Little Girl*, a flop melodrama that died after sixteen performances. (In 1961, Fonda's easy-rider son, Peter, made his debut in *Blood, Sweat and Stanley Poole*.) In 1978, Fonda made his last Broadway appearance in *First Monday in October* as a Supreme Court justice appalled when the president appoints the first woman to sit on the court.

It played for three sold-out months; then Fonda, ever the trouper, moved on with it to Chicago. He had to stop there. A hip ailment, subsequently diagnosed as cancer, finally ended his touring.

But not his spirit. In the winter of 1981, after making the only film that ever won him an Oscar, *On Golden Pond*, the trouper was back on stage. He moved unsteadily but acted with sureness, again in regional theater, having begun there fifty-six years earlier in *You and I* and now taking that final bow in *Showdown at the Adobe Motel*.

He was still an actor's actor, one who rarely reached outside his range, one who knew what he could do best and did it.

"Who knows," Henry Fonda once mused. "Maybe if I'd been smart enough and always had the ambition and begun when really a young man to study, I might have the equipment to be the serious actor Olivier is.

"I don't mean the talent, I mean the equipment. I know my limits."

To many, however, Fonda's acting had no limits. At the Kennedy Center Honors for Fonda in 1979, Josh Logan said: "I've seen actors come and go . . . but as far as I'm concerned, Henry Fonda is the greatest actor in the world."

Henry Fonda receives a ham and a piece of land after being named the winner of the 1948 Barter Theater Award for "outstanding performance by an American born actor." The ham was presented to Fonda by Robert Porterfield, the director of the Barter Theater of Abingdon, Virginia. The deed for an acre of land was presented to him by actress Helen Hayes, who was the 1947 award winner. Fonda won the honor for his performance in the play *Mister Roberts*.

Fonda getting ready to go on stage in *Mister Roberts* at Broadway's Alvin Theater in 1948.

The Game of Life and Death (1929). Theatre Guild production starring Claude Rains. Fonda was a $15-a-week walk-on, for six weeks.

I Loved You Wednesday (1932). Romantic comedy-drama starring Humphrey Bogart as an architect torn between his wealthy wife (Rose Hobart) and the pretty girl (Frances Fuller) he knew and loved during his student days in Paris. Fonda played a bar patron who had no lines; he sat opposite a teen-aged Arlene Francis. Others in cast: Henry O'Neill, Jane Seymour.

Forsaking All Others (1933). Comedy about the tribulations of the bride jilted at the altar. Tallulah Bankhead starred as the bride, Fred Keating as her faithful friend. Fonda was Keating's understudy. Others in cast: Ilka Chase, Cora Witherspoon, Barbara O'Neil, Anderson Lawler, Harlan Briggs, Donald MacDonald, Roger Sterns, Millicent Hanley, Nancy Ryan.

New Faces (1934). A revue, the first of many produced by Leonard Sillman. Cast included Fonda, Imogene Coca, Nancy Hamilton.

The Farmer Takes a Wife (1934). A sentimental, occasionally salty comedy about life along the Erie Canal in the 1800s. Fonda, in his first Broadway starring role, played a virtuous farm boy in love with the daughter (June Walker) of a river-boat clan. Others in cast: Margaret Hamilton, Herb Williams, Joseph Sweeney, Robert Ross, Kate Mayhew, Gibbs Penrose.

Blow Ye Winds (1937). Comedy-drama about the romance of an amiable sailor and a woman scientist. Fonda played the sailor. Others in cast: Blaine Cordner, Doris Dalton, Edgar Barrier, Edgar Stehli.

Mister Roberts (1948). World War II navy comedy-drama about the men of a navy cargo ship in a safe area of the Pacific. Fonda starred in the title role. Others in cast: David Wayne, William Harrigan, Robert Keith, Jocelyn Brando, Ralph Meeker, Harvey Lembeck, Rusty Lane, Steven Hill, Murray Hamilton, Marshall Jamison.

Point of No Return (1951). Drama about an unhappy Manhattan banker from a small New England town. Fonda starred as the banker. Others in cast: Frank Conroy, Phil Arthur, Frances Bavier, Colin Keith-Johnston, Leora Dana, John Cromwell, Robert Ross, Patricia

The Caine Mutiny Court Martial (1954). Herman Wouk's dramatization of the court-martial scenes in his best-selling novel *The Caine Mutiny*. Fonda starred as

I want to drink a toast to you, Mr. Keefer. From the beginning, you hated the Navy. You thought up the whole idea, and you kept your skirts all starched and clean. Steve Maryk will be remembered as a mutineer—but you! You'll publish a novel, you'll make a million bucks, you'll marry a movie star, and, for the rest of your life, you'll have to live with your conscience, if you have any. Now, here's to the real author of "The Caine Mutiny." Here's to you, Mr. Keefer.

As Barney Greenwald in *The Caine Mutiny Court Martial*

Henry Fonda in a pensive scene from *The Caine Mutiny Court Martial* at Broadway's Plymouth Theatre in 1954.

Henry Fonda appears with Leora Dana in the same production, presented by Leland Hayward.

Actor John Cromwell and Henry Fonda as they appear together in Paul Osborne's play *Point of No Return* in 1952.

With actor John Hodiak in *The Caine Mutiny*.

Another scene from *The Caine Mutiny*.

Actress Olivia De Havilland and Henry Fonda appear backstage at New York's Barrymore Theater after their opening in the play *A Gift of Time* in 1962. The drama was written and directed by Garson Kanin.

defense lawyer Lt. Barney Greenwald. Others in cast: Lloyd Nolan, John Hodiak, and James Baumgarner, later a star on television as James Garner.

Two for the Seesaw (1958). Two-character comedy-drama by William Gibson about a kooky Jewish girl (Anne Bancroft) in love with a midwestern lawyer (Fonda).

Silent Night, Lonely Night (1959). Drama by Robert (*Tea and Sympathy*) Anderson about two lonely people (Fonda and Barbara Bel Geddes) who find love Christmas Eve in a New England inn. Others in cast: Bill Berger, Lois Nettleton, Eda Heinemann, Peter de Vise.

Critic's Choice (1960). Ira Levin comedy about a New York drama critic (Fonda) forced to review a terrible play by his wife (Georgann Johnson). Others in cast: Mildred Natwick, Murray Hamilton, Virginia Gilmore, Eddie Hodges, Billie Allen.

A Gift of Time (1962). Grim study of a man (Fonda) dying of cancer; in the climax, he slashes his wrists with the razor his compassionate wife (Olivia De Havilland) has given him. Others in cast: Joseph Campanella, Philip Huston, Guy Sorel, Marian Seldes.

Generation (1965). A comedy about an uptight advertising man (Fonda) upset by the marriage of his daughter to an antiestablishment beatnik. Others in cast: Dolores Sutton, Roscoe Lee Browne, Lonny Chapman, Ann Harding, Paul Stevens, Tim O'Connor.

Our Town (1969). Revival of Thornton Wilder's turn-of-the-century tale of life, love, and death in a New England village. Fonda starred as the narrator. Others in cast: Margaret Hamilton, Ed Begley, Harvey Evans, Mildred Natwick, Elizabeth Hartman, Irene Tedrow, John Randolph, John Beal, Thomas Coley.

Clarence Darrow (1974). One-man drama, by David Rintels, starring Fonda as Clarence Darrow, famous American trial lawyer and major figure in landmark cases.

First Monday in October (1978). Drama about a crusty U.S. Supreme Court justice (Fonda) upset when the president appoints the first woman (Jane Alexander) ever to sit on the court. Also with Larry Gates. (*New York Times* critic Walter Kerr said Fonda "emerges so unmistakably as something more than a reliable actor, transforming himself into a phenomenon, a legend, before your eyes.")

Opposite: Henry Fonda in *Generation*, a comedy that opened on Broadway in September 1965.

Fonda is the only member of the cast in this one-man play, which opened at London's Picadilly Theatre in July 1975.

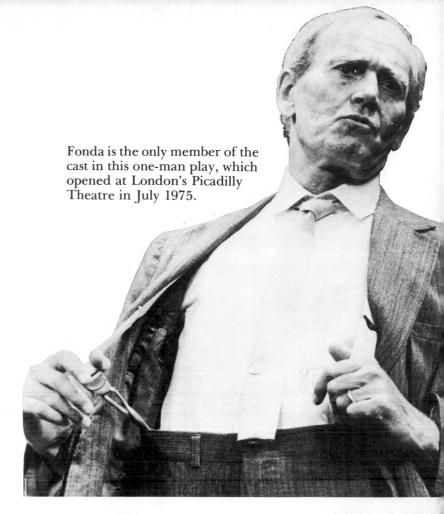

Henry Fonda prepares for his role as the famed American lawyer *Clarence Darrow* in Chicago, June 1974.

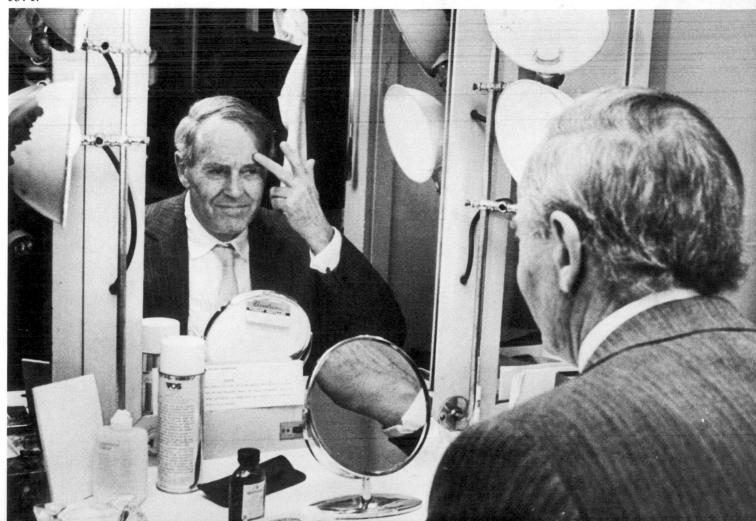

Henry Fonda in two poses from *First Monday in October,* which opened on Broadway in 1978 (*above and opposite*).

Here he appears backstage with *First Monday in October* costar Jane Alexander.

ON THE
BIG SCREEN

Henry Fonda is photographed as he leaves the Regency Theatre in New York City after receiving the Regency's "Award of Merit" in November of 1978. Two of Fonda's films, *The Grapes of Wrath* and *The Ox-Bow Incident,* are listed on the marquee behind him.

It has been said that Henry Fonda retained his star status for some fifty years by taking virtually any movie role that came along.

Indeed, the Fonda credits are weighty: more than eighty theatrical motion pictures, two television series, several television movies and plays, many appearances as host or narrator of television shows or specials, and a televised live play. All that plus seventeen Broadway appearances and numerous regional, community, and stock theater roles.

But merely looking at numbers ignores the fact that Fonda's enduring star power had as much to do with the quality of his work as it did with its remarkable volume. Critics often groped for new superlatives to describe Fonda's contribution to movies such as *Young Mr. Lincoln, The Grapes of Wrath, My Darling Clementine, Mister Roberts, 12 Angry Men, The Cheyenne Social Club,* and *Sometimes a Great Notion.*

By the 1970s, as often happens to aging actors, Fonda roles often were little more than cameos or supporting parts. But old age, untypically, also brought several of the most rewarding roles of his distinguished career: "Gideon's Trumpet" (TV movie) in 1979; *The Oldest Living Graduate* (live TV play) in 1980; "Summer Solstice" (TV movie) in 1981; and, climactically, his Academy-Award-winning portrayal of an octogenarian facing death in *On Golden Pond.*

The movies Fonda appeared in often were far from top-drawer. He made no secret of his revulsion for a series of projects he made at Fox in the late 1930s and early 1940s while under contract. But Fonda's acting usually triumphed over the silly writing or poor production or direction.

"*Young Mr. Lincoln* is a personal triumph for Mr. Fonda," *Newsweek* said of that 1939 role despite the misgivings it and others had about the movie itself. By the time he portrayed John Steinbeck's Tom Joad in *The Grapes of Wrath*, Fonda's simplicity of style, of directness, of emotion, had become his "salt-of-the-earth American" trademarks. That movie brought him an Academy Award nomination for Best Actor and abundant critical acclaim: "Fonda, for example, has never been better . . ." said Howard Barnes in the New York *Herald Tribune*. "Henry Fonda's Tom Joad is precisely the hot-tempered, resolute saturnine chap Mr. Steinbeck had in mind. . . ." said Frank Nugent, *New York Times* critic.

Yet in 1941's *The Lady Eve* with Barbara Stanwyck, critics were still surprised at Fonda's range. *Newsweek* praised Fonda and Miss Stanwyck for "the ease and high humor with which this pair take to light comedy."

Even from a public accustomed to Fonda "the hero," he drew praise in one of his few unsympathetic characterizations, that of a stiff-backed U.S. Cavalry officer in *Fort Apache. Time* magazine said the role was "aptly played."

The role for which he is most identified, however, surely is his Lt. Doug Roberts in *Mister Roberts. Time* noted his "honest-injun" appeal. Fonda "has caught every nuance appropriate to the nation's big brother." Lee Rogow, in *Saturday Review*, acknowledged the distinctive Fonda style when he said, "Fonda's performance in the role is superb. It is spare, quiet, absolutely sure."

In the 1956 version of Leo Tolstoy's epic *War and Peace, Time* savaged most of the acting in the movie but spotlighted Fonda's role as Pierre.

Henry Fonda's leanness at first seems all wrong for the massive, moon-faced, soul-tortured Pierre. But Fonda builds beautifully into his part, using a physical clumsiness as a counterpoise to his soaring spirit, making his rages seem the more terrible since they flash out from passivity. As he strug-

Henry Fonda and Cloris Leachman rehearse on stage at Southern Methodist University in Dallas, Texas, for an April 7, 1980, live television broadcast of *The Oldest Living Graduate*. The play, written by the late Preston Jones, was the first live drama on NBC in eighteen years.

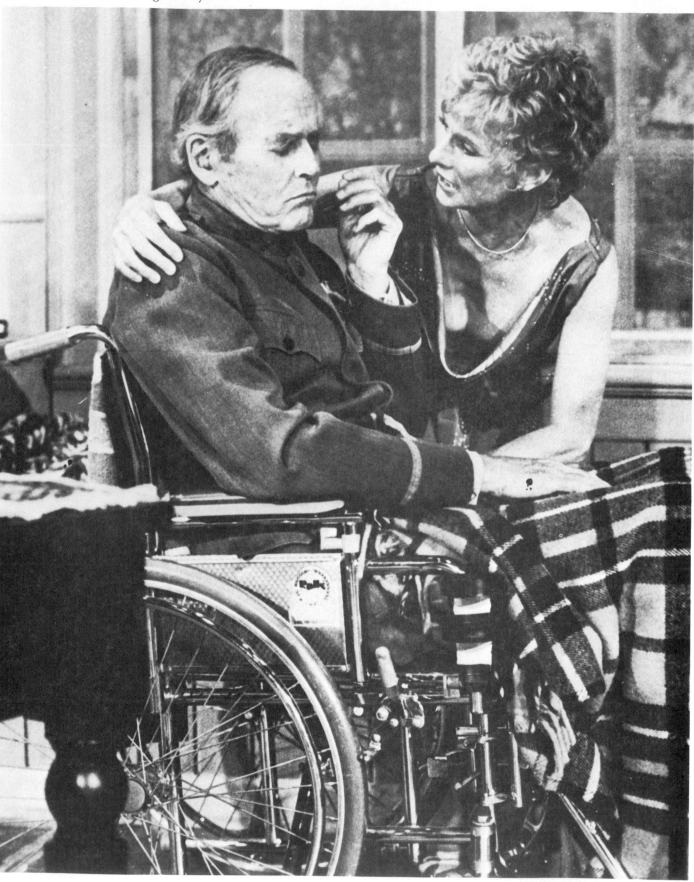

Henry Fonda blows out the candles on his birthday cake at the Wilshire Theater in Los Angeles on May 16, 1980. With Fonda are his wife, Shirlee, at left, son, Peter, and daughter, Jane. Fonda, 75 years old, was appearing in the stage version of *The Oldest Living Graduate*. The cast and crew of the play are also on hand to celebrate Fonda's birthday.

gles for the answers to the great questions (Why does a man live? Why does he kill? Who owns his loyalty?), Fonda acts to the very limit of his considerable powers, and sometimes gives the impression of being the only man in the huge cast who has read the book.

Fonda often played men of conscience battling their own weaknesses while being sucked into the whirlpools of social-political reality. Regarding his role in the screen version of Gore Vidal's *Best Man*, Stanley Kauffmann in the *New Republic* said: "Henry Fonda could play [secretary of state candidate William] Russell in his sleep, but has refused to do so; it is an alert, humorous, rueful performance."

Time, appraising *Sometimes a Great Notion* (1971), was very impressed by Fonda's portrait of the head of an Oregon lumberjack family. In a cast that included Paul Newman and Richard Jaeckel, who was nominated for a Best Supporting Actor Oscar in this movie, *Time* said: "Fonda, as the old man, simply beats everyone cold. He has a death scene that must stand among the best work of a lifetime filled with superb film acting."

By 1967, Fonda had climbed to among the top-twenty box-office attractions on a *Variety* listing. Through the 1970s, he lent his box-office appeal to a string of run-of-the-mill, star-studded extravaganzas such as *Midway*, *The Swarm*, *Fedora*, and *Meteor*.

On television, he had a fairly substantial role on "Roots: The Next Generation," but also made some forgettable exploitation vehicles such as "Tentacles," "The Great Smokey Roadblock," and "City on Fire."

In 1981, he received an honorary Academy Award, which may have represented some contrition on the part of Academy voters for overlooking him for so long.

But it seemed the best was saved for last: *On Golden Pond*, in which he teamed for the first time with Katharine Hepburn and his daughter, Jane Fonda. As Norman Thayer, he won an avalanche of accolades and his first Academy Award for acting in a story about a man approaching death and of a father making amends with his estranged daughter. The film had eerie parallels with Fonda's real life family situation.

In his *Time* magazine piece, Richard Schickel said Fonda:

has had to wait until the end of his life for the part of his life. As Norman he is able to bring together, in a single character, the two main strands of his talent. The old gentleman's character is grounded on the main line of Fonda's star career. The fundamental decency and intelligence that were basic to the likes of Tom Joad and Mr. Roberts still infuse his presence . . . Without raising his voice he gives a bravura performance as he moves from depressed withdrawal to momentary rages, from the struggle to express affection to the struggle not to express it, lest it be mistaken for weakness.

In the movie's final scene, Ethel Thayer (Miss Hepburn) says to her husband, "Norman, this is the first time I've really felt we're going to die." Norman replies, "I've known it all along."

A young Fonda appears as Dan Barrow in the 1935
film version of *The Farmer Takes a Wife*.

The Farmer Takes a Wife (1935), Twentieth Century-Fox. Victor Fleming, director. With Janet Gaynor, Charles Bickford, Slim Summerville, Andy Devine, Roger Imhof, Jane Withers, Margaret Hamilton. Fonda's film debut, recreating in this romantic drama the role of Dan Harrow he originated on Broadway.

Way Down East (1935), Twentieth Century-Fox. Henry King, director. With Rochelle Hudson, Slim Summerville, Edward Trevor, Margaret Hamilton, Andy Devine, Spring Byington. A remake of the D. W. Griffith silent, with Fonda playing David Bartlett. The critics' blasts against this tear-jerker threatened to melt the ice floes across which Rochelle Hudson fled in emulation of Griffith's famous heroine, Lillian Gish, but Fonda fared well.

I Dream Too Much (1935), RKO. John Cromwell, director. With Eric Blore, Osgood Perkins, and Lucille Ball. French girl singer (real-life diva Lily Pons) marries American composer (Fonda).

The Trail of the Lonesome Pine (1936), Paramount. Henry Hathaway, director. With Fred MacMurray, Sylvia Sidney, Nigel Bruce, Beulah Bondi, Spanky McFarland. This remake of a well-known hillbilly feud yarn was the first outdoor movie to be shot in three-strip Technicolor. Fonda was Dave Tolliver.

The Moon's Our Home (1936), Paramount. William A. Seiter, director. With Margaret Sullavan (Fonda's ex-wife), Charles Butterworth, Beulah Bondi, Margaret Hamilton, Walter Brennan. Boosted by Dorothy Parker's glossy rewrite, this then-fashionable screwball farce gave Fonda his first—and one of his best—comedic roles as an adventurer-writer in love with a temperamental starlet.

Spendthrift (1936), Paramount. Directed by Raoul Walsh. With Pat Peterson, Mary Brian, George Barbier, Edward Brophy. A forgettable comedy—that Fonda claims he never saw—about a boy millionaire.

Wings of the Morning (1937), Twentieth Century-Fox. Harold Schuster, director. With Annabella, Stewart Rome, John McCormack, Leslie Banks, Irene Vanbrugh, Helen Haye. The critics used terms like "charming," "delightful," and "refreshing" to describe this English romance. French chanteuse Annabella masqueraded as a boy to disguise her royal blood, while Fonda was her nobleman-lover.

You Only Live Once (1937), United Artists. Fritz Lang, director. With Sylvia Sidney, Barton MacLane, Jean Dixon, Jerome Cowan, William Gargan. In Fritz Lang's dark masterpiece, based partly on the story of outlaws Bonnie Parker and Clyde Barrow, Fonda and Miss Sidney play a star-crossed couple.

Slim (1937), Warner Bros. Ray Enright, director. With Pat O'Brien, Margaret Lindsay, Stuart Erwin, J. Farrell MacDonald, Jane Wyman. "Heart-pounding" thrills surrounding a team of high-tension wire electricians, with taut action sequences, for which Warner Bros. was noted.

That Certain Woman (1937), Warner Bros. Edmund Goulding, director. With Bette Davis, Ian Hunter, Anita Louise, Donald Crisp, Katherine Alexander, Mary Philips. Fonda stood in the shadow of Miss Davis, a gangster's widow trying to go straight.

I Met My Love Again (1938), United Artists. Joshua Logan, Arthur Ripley, directors. With Joan Bennett, Alan Marshal, Dorothy Stickney, Dame May Whitty, Alan Baxter. This conventional romance featured Fonda as biology professor Ives Towner, whose life is disrupted by ex-love, Miss Bennett.

Jezebel (1938), Warner Bros. William Wyler, director. With Bette Davis, George Brent, Margaret Lindsay, Fay Bainter, Richard Cromwell, Donald Crisp, Henry O'Neill, John Litel, Spring Byington, Eddie Anderson. Miss Davis won a Best Actress Oscar for her role as a Southern belle who dared to wear red to an all-white ball. Fonda played her beau, Preston Dillard. Miss Bainter won a Best Supporting Actress Oscar. Other Oscar nominations: Best Picture; Best Cinematography, Ernest Haller; Best Score, Max Steiner.

Blockade (1938), United Artists. William Dieterle, director. With Madeleine Carroll, Leo Carrillo, John Halliday, Vladimir Sokoloff, Robert Warwick, Reginald Denny. Fonda plays a young farmer who takes up arms to defend his land, while Miss Carroll is a beautiful spy in a Spanish Civil War-type setting. The movie was controversial politically and critically unacclaimed but won Oscar nominations for John Howard Lawson's original screenplay and Werner Janssen's original score.

Spawn of the North (1938), Paramount. Henry Hathaway, director. With George Raft, Dorothy Lamour, John Barrymore, Akim Tamiroff, Duncan Renaldo, Louise Platt, Lynne Overman. Fonda is the all-American hero pitted against Russian salmon poachers in a lusty tale set on the iceberg-filled Alaskan frontier.

The Mad Miss Manton (1938), RKO. Leigh Jason, director. With Barbara Stanwyck, Sam Levene, Frances Mercer, Stanley Ridges, Hattie McDaniel. Comedy-thriller full of popular 1930s zaniness. Fonda plays a skeptical newspaper columnist who doesn't believe there's been a murder.

Jesse James (1939), Twentieth Century-Fox. Henry King, director. Tyrone Power, Nancy Kelly, Jane Darwell, Randolph Scott, Slim Summerville, Brian Donlevy, John Carradine, Donald Meek, Henry Hull. Fonda played brother Frank to Tyrone Power's Jesse in the classic version of the train-robbing James brothers. He was well cast as the tobacco-chewing sodbuster-turned-outlaw.

Let Us Live (1939), Columbia. John Brahm, director. With Maureen O'Sullivan, Ralph Bellamy, Alan Baxter. Based on a true incident, Fonda plays a taxi driver on trial for murder in a case of mistaken identity.

The Story of Alexander Graham Bell (**The Modern Miracle** in Great Britain) (1939), Twentieth Century-Fox.

Fonda—the personification of the young Illinois lawyer.

Fonda in one of his most famous roles, in the 1939 film *Young Mr. Lincoln,* directed by John Ford.

Here Fonda appears in his now-legendary role of Tom Joad in *The Grapes of Wrath*, released in 1940.

Irving Cummings, director. With Don Ameche, Loretta Young, Charles Coburn, Gene Lockhart, Spring Byington. Fonda plays the great inventor's assistant, Thomas Watson.

Young Mr. Lincoln (1939), Twentieth Century-Fox. John Ford, director. With Alice Brady, Marjorie Weaver, Arleen Whelan, Eddie Collins, Richard Cromwell, Donald Meek, Eddie Quillan. Fonda, in heavy makeup, was the personification of the young Illinois lawyer. Lamar Trotti was Oscar-nominated for his original story.

Drums Along the Mohawk (1939), Twentieth Century-Fox. John Ford, director. With Claudette Colbert, Edna May Oliver, Eddie Collins, John Carradine, Ward Bond. A Revolutionary War-era adventure pitting settlers against the Indians, told in director John Ford's muscular, visual style. Edna May Oliver received a Best Supporting Actress Oscar nomination.

The Grapes of Wrath (1940), Twentieth Century-Fox. John Ford, director. With Jane Darwell, John Carradine, Charley Grapewin, Dorris Bowden, Russell Simpson, Zeffie Tilbury, Eddie Quillan, John Qualen, O. Z. Whitehead. Fonda, in a now-legendary portrayal of John Steinbeck's itinerant farmer Tom Joad, won his first Best Actor Oscar nomination but lost to pal Jimmy Stewart (*The Philadelphia Story*). John Ford won the Best Director Oscar, while Jane Darwell took the Best Supporting Actress nod. The film was nominated for Best Picture and for Nunnally Johnson's riveting screenplay, while the critics grasped for new superlatives.

Lillian Russell (1940), Twentieth Century-Fox. Irving Cummings, director. With Alice Faye, Don Ameche, Edward Arnold, Warren William, Leo Carrillo, Nigel Bruce, Eddie Foy, Jr. Fonda was a romantic lead in the biofilm of the famous 1890s entertainer.

The Return of Frank James (1940), Twentieth Century-Fox. Fritz Lang, director. With Gene Tierney, Jackie Cooper, Henry Hull, Donald Meek, John Carradine, J. Edward Bromberg. A sequel to the big-box-office *Jesse James*. Fonda won critical approval in Fritz Lang's moody Western.

Chad Hanna (1940), Twentieth Century-Fox. Henry King, director. With Dorothy Lamour, Linda Darnell, John Carradine, Guy Kibbee, Jane Darwell. Fonda, playing the country boy again, joins the circus in up-state New York in the 1840s.

The Lady Eve (1941), Paramount. Preston Sturges, director. With Barbara Stanwyck, Charles Coburn, Eugene Pallette, Wiliam Demarest, Melville Cooper, Eric Blore. On loan-out to Paramount, Fonda, not noted for comedic talent, portrayed a rich bachelor to great effect. Equally against-type casting was Miss Stanwyck's temptress. It is slapstick and high artifice that won Monckton Hoffe an Oscar nomination for his original story.

In the 1943 film *The Immortal Sergeant,* Fonda plays
the timid writer Corporal Spence.

Hangin's any man's business that's around.

As Gil Carter in *The Ox-Bow Incident*

Wild Geese Calling (1941), Twentieth Century-Fox, John Brahm, director. With Joan Bennett, Warren William, Barton MacLane, Russell Simpson, Ona Munson. A semi-Western about a young Oregon adventurer who marries a woman he suspects of a shady past.

You Belong to Me (1941), Columbia. Wesley Ruggles, director. With Barbara Stanwyck, Edgar Buchanan, Roger Clark, Melville Cooper, Ruth Donnelly. A lightweight romance. Fonda, a playboy, is jealous of his doctor wife.

The Male Animal (1942), Warner Bros. Elliott Nugent, director. With Olivia De Havilland, Jack Carson, Joan Leslie, Eugene Pallette, Don DeFore, Hattie McDaniel, Herbert Anderson. Based on the Broadway play, Fonda portrays staid Professor Tommy Turner, whose wife (De Havilland) falls for a football star (Carson). Fonda later revived the role in a summer stock production with daughter Jane.

Rings on Her Fingers (1942), Twentieth Century-Fox. Rouben Mamoulian, director. With Gene Tierney, Laird Cregar, Spring Byington, Henry Stephenson. A lady con artist falls for her victim, a naive young man.

The Magnificent Dope (1942), Twentieth Century-Fox. Walter Lang, director. With Lynn Bari, Don Ameche, Edward Everett Horton, Frank Orth. A local yokel, brought to New York as a success-school publicity stunt, gets the best of the city folks.

Tales of Manhattan (1942), Twentieth Century-Fox. Julien Duvivier, director. With Charles Boyer, Rita Hayworth, Charles Laughton, Edward G. Robinson, Eugene Pallette, Ginger Rogers, Cesar Romero, Elsa Lanchester, George Sanders, Paul Robeson, Ethel Waters. Fonda appeared in one part of this episodic story of a suit of tails passed from owner to owner.

The Big Street (1942), RKO. Irving Reis, director. With Lucille Ball, Barton MacLane, Eugene Pallette, Agnes Moorehead, Ozzie Nelson and His Orchestra. Fonda, a Broadway night club waiter, falls for an ill-tempered, crippled singer. A sentimental Damon Runyon fairy tale.

The Immortal Sergeant (1943), Twentieth Century-Fox. John Stahl, director. With Maureen O'Hara, Thomas Mitchell, Allyn Joslyn, Reginald Gardiner, Melville Cooper. Fonda plays Corporal Colin Spence, a timid writer who inspires his men during the North African campaign. Fonda had entered the navy by the time this movie was released.

The Ox-Bow Incident (1943), Twentieth Century-Fox. William Wellman, director. With Henry Morgan, Dana Andrews, Anthony Quinn, Frank Conroy, Jane Darwell, Mary Beth Hughes. A cowboy cannot prevent the hanging of three men lynched for murder.

My Darling Clementine (1946), Twentieth Century-Fox. John Ford, director. With Victor Mature, Walter Brennan, Linda Darnell, Cathy Downs, Ward Bond, Alan Mowbray, John Ireland. In his first postwar film, Fonda portrays Marshall Wyatt Earp in frontier Tombstone, Arizona, in what many critics consider director John Ford's best.

The Long Night (1947), RKO. Anatole Litvak, director. With Barbara Bel Geddes, Vincent Price, Ann Dvorak, Queenie Smith, Elisha Cook, Jr. A fugitive barricades himself against police after he murders a love rival.

The Fugitive (1947), RKO. John Ford, director. With Dolores Del Rio, Pedro Armendariz, J. Carrol Naish, Leo Carrillo, Ward Bond, Robert Armstrong, John Qualen. Fonda is a runaway priest in an anticlerical South American country.

Daisy Kenyon (1947), Twentieth Century-Fox. Otto Preminger, director. With Joan Crawford, Dana Andrews, Ruth Warrick, Martha Stewart, Peggy Ann Garner. New York fashion designer Joan Crawford must decide between marriage to Fonda or an affair with Andrews. Fonda wins.

On Our Merry Way (released in Britain as *A Miracle Can Happen*) (1948), United Artists. King Vidor, Leslie Fenton, directors. With James Stewart, Paulette Goddard, Burgess Meredith, Fred MacMurray, Dorothy Lamour, Victor Moore, William Demarest, Dorothy Ford. Episodic story, with various casts, in which reporter digs up human-interest yarns.

Henry Fonda (seated at left) appears in the 1948 movie *Fort Apache*. Next to Fonda is costar John Wayne.

In the 1955 film *War and Peace,* Fonda stars with Audrey Hepburn. His shy, questioning portrayal of the intellectual bumbler Pierre charmed critics.

Fort Apache (1948), RKO. John Ford, director. With John Wayne, Shirley Temple, Pedro Armendariz, Ward Bond, Victor McLaglen, John Agar, Irene Rich, Guy Kibbee. Fonda plays a by-the-book U.S. Cavalry colonel. It was against type for Fonda, who by the time of the film's release was playing a much different military man, *Mister Roberts*, on stage. Wayne won the acclaim here.

Jigsaw (1949), United Artists. Fletcher Markle, director. With Franchot Tone, Jean Wallace, Myron McCormick, Marc Lawrence, Marlene Dietrich. Fonda was one of many of several guest stars doing cameos.

Mister Roberts (1955), Warner Bros. John Ford, Mervyn LeRoy directors. With James Cagney, William Powell, Jack Lemmon, Betsy Palmer, Ward Bond, Nick Adams, Harry Carey, Jr., Phil Carey, Ken Curtis. Perhaps only Fonda's Tom Joad in *Grapes of Wrath* can rival the acclaim accorded his *Mister Roberts*, which he trademarked in the enormously popular stage play. Fonda, who had taken a long break from movies for the stage, still was a sensation here on screen.

War and Peace (1956), Paramount. King Vidor, director. With Audrey Hepburn, Mel Ferrer, Vittorio Gassman, John Mills, Herbert Lom, Oscar Homolka, Anita Ekberg, Helmut Dantine. Fonda was the first to agree he was miscast physically as the intellectual bumbler Pierre. But his shy, questioning portrayal beguiled the critics, anyway. Academy Award nominations went to King Vidor's direction and Jack Cardiff's cinematography.

The Wrong Man (1956), Warner Bros. Alfred Hitchcock, director. With Vera Miles, Anthony Quayle, Harold J. Stone, Nehemiah Persoff. Fonda plays the innocent victim of circumstances in a true story about a musician fingered for murder. Not one of Hitchcock's best.

The Tin Star (1957), Paramount. Anthony Mann, director. With Anthony Perkins, Betsy Palmer, Michel Ray, Neville Brand, John McIntire. Filled with overtones of *High Noon*, Fonda plays an ex-sheriff who takes a young lawman (Perkins) under his wing in a film with unusual depth for the genre. Oscar nominations for original story (Barney Slater and Joel Kane) and screenplay (Dudley Nichols).

12 Angry Men (1957), United Artists. Sidney Lumet, director. With Lee J. Cobb, E. G. Marshall, Jack Warden, Martin Balsam, Ed Begley, John Fiedler, Jack Klugman, Edward Binns, Joseph Sweeney, George Voscovec, Robert Webber. Fonda coproduced this taut drama about a man trying to convince his fellow jurors to acquit a boy accused of killing his father. Although a

Fonda as he appears in the 1955 film *Mr. Roberts,* in which he recreated his classic stage role.

Opposite: Fonda as he appears in the 1963 film *Spencer's Mountain*.

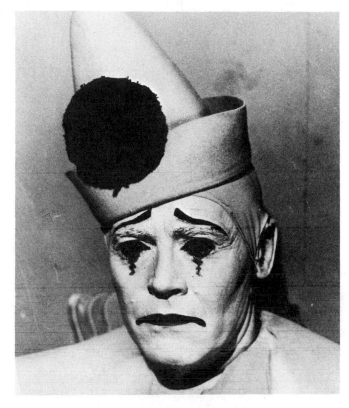

In the title role of the 1959 film *The Man Who Understood Women*, Fonda goes through a dizzying array of impersonations as a wunderkind Hollywood producer.

box-office failure, the film was a critical success and won Oscar nominations for Best Picture, Director (Sidney Lumet) and Screenplay Adaptation (Reginald Rose).

Stage Struck (1958), RKO. Sidney Lumet, director. With Susan Strasberg, Herbert Marshall, Joan Greenwood, Christopher Plummer. Fonda plays producer Lewis Easton, but the tribulations of hungry young New York actors had been done better elsewhere.

Warlock (1959), Twentieth Century-Fox. Edward Dmytryk, director. With Richard Widmark, Anthony Quinn, Dorothy Malone, Dolores Michaels, Wallace Ford, Tom Drake, Richard Arlen, De Forest Kelly. A better-than-average Western that led to Fonda's first television series "The Deputy" (1959–1961), in which he played Marshal Simon Fry.

The Man Who Understood Women (1959), Twentieth Century-Fox. Nunnally Johnson, director. With Leslie Caron, Myron McCormick, Cesare Danova, Marcel Dallo, Conrad Nagel. A film in which Fonda, in a serio-comic role, goes through a dizzying array of impersonations as a wunderkind Hollywood producer.

Advise and Consent (1962), Columbia. Otto Preminger, director. With Don Murray, Charles Laughton, Walter Pidgeon, Lew Ayres, Edward Andrews, Burgess Meredith, George Grizzard, Gene Tierney, Franchot Tone. As an unpopular choice for U.S. secretary of state, Fonda has little to do in this political melodrama.

The Longest Day (1962), Twentieth Century-Fox. Andrew Marton, Ken Annakin, Bernhard Wicki, directors. With John Wayne, Robert Mitchum, Robert Ryan, Rod Steiger, Robert Wagner, Richard Burton, Sal Mineo, Stuart Whitman, Roddy McDowall, Red Buttons, Kenneth More, Peter Lawford, Sean Connery, Curt Jurgens, Jeffery Hunter, Gerd Froebe, Christopher Lee and many, many others. Fonda turned in a brief appearance in this cameo-laden D-day epic.

How the West Was Won (1963), M-G-M-Cinerama. Henry Hathaway, John Ford, George Marshall, directors. With Spencer Tracy, Carroll Baker, Lee J. Cobb, Carolyn Jones, Debbie Reynolds, Karl Malden, Gregory Peck, George Peppard, Robert Preston, James Stewart, Eli Wallach, John Wayne, Richard Widmark, Walter Brennan, Andy Devine. A patchwork of Western movie clichés, the big-screen Cinerama process, and dozens of stars couldn't save this film. Fonda, in a small role, played a shaggy buffalo hunter.

Spencer's Mountain (1963), Warner Bros. Delmar Daves, director. With Maureen O'Hara, James MacArthur, Donald Crisp, Wally Cox, Mimsy Farmer, Lillian

Susan Strasberg stars with Fonda in the 1959 film *Stage Struck*. Fonda played producer Lewis Easton in this RKO movie.

Henry Fonda and British actress Margaret Leighton
relax between scenes on the Hollywood set of *The
Best Man* in November 1963. Fonda played the role
of a presidential candidate, and Miss Leighton
played his wife.

Fail Safe, released in 1964, is a frighteningly convincing portrait of nuclear brinksmanship. Fonda is seen here in the role of a U.S. president who must destroy New York City in retaliation for the American bombing of Moscow.

Bronson. Backwoods hokum that turned out much better as television's "The Waltons."

The Best Man (1964), United Artists. Franklin Schaffner, director. With Cliff Robertson, Margaret Leighton, Lee Tracy, Edie Adams, Shelley Berman, Ann Sothern, Gene Raymond, Mahalia Jackson, Kevin McCarthy. Based on Gore Vidal's incisive play, this was political melodrama at its best. Fonda played an Adlai Stevenson-like former secretary of state. Lee Tracy was Oscar-nominated as Best Supporting Actor.

Fail Safe (1964), Columbia. Sidney Lumet, director. With Dan O'Herlihy, Walter Matthau, Frank Overton, Fritz Weaver, Edward Binns, Larry Hagman. Fonda plays a U.S. president who must destroy New York City in retaliation for the American bombing of Moscow. A frighteningly convincing portrait of nuclear brinksmanship, it suffered by comparison with Stanley Kubrick's brilliant *Dr. Strangelove*, which Columbia released the year before.

Sex and the Single Girl (1964), Warner Bros. Richard Quine, director. With Natalie Wood, Lauren Bacall, Tony Curtis, Mel Ferrer, Edward Everett Horton, Fran Jeffries. Fonda and Bacall were generally well liked in this frothy project about a lady sex researcher.

The Rounders (1965), M-G-M. Burt Kennedy, director. With Glenn Ford, Sue Anne Langdon, Hope Holiday, Chill Wills, Denver Pyle, Edgar Buchanan. An offbeat, nostalgic Western, with Fonda and Ford delighting everyone with their past-their-prime cowpoke characterizations.

In Harm's Way (1965), Paramount. Otto Preminger, director. With John Wayne, Kirk Douglas, Patricia Neal, Dana Andrews, Tom Tryon, Burgess Meredith, Brandon de Wilde, Stanley Holloway, Jill Haworth, Franchot Tone, George Kennedy, Hugh O'Brien, Slim Pickens, Larry Hagman. Limp post-Pearl Harbor naval action, with a star-studded cast and Fonda in a small role as an admiral. Oscar nominated for Loyal Griggs's cinematography.

Battle of the Bulge (1965), Warner Bros. Ken Annakin, director. With Robert Shaw, Robert Ryan, Dana Andrews, George Montgomery, Charles Bronson, Telly Savalas, Pier Angeli, Barbara Werle. Another all-star spectacular, with Fonda as a lieutenant colonel wading through a distorted re-enactment of the famous World War II battle.

A Big Hand for the Little Lady (1966), Warner Bros. Fielder Cook, director. With Joanne Woodward, Jason Robards, Paul Ford, Kevin McCarthy, Charles Bickford, Burgess Meredith, John Qualen. Tense poker-game drama in a Western saloon, with Fonda as an inveterate gambler.

In 1965, Henry Fonda works on location in West Berlin for the filming of *The Dirty Game*. Fonda portrays a Soviet intelligence officer in the film.

The Dirty Game (1966). American International Pictures. Terrence Young, Christian-Jaque, Carlo Lizzani, directors. With Robert Ryan, Vittorio Gassman, Annie Girardot. Another episodic movie, with Fonda playing a Russian spy in his segment.

Welcome to Hard Times (1967), M-G-M. Burt Kennedy, director. With Janice Rule, Keenan Wynn, Janis Paige, John Anderson, Warren Oates, Edgar Buchanan, Aldo Ray, Elisha Cook, Jr. Fonda as an anti-hero in a "symbolic" Western.

Firecreek (1968), Warner Bros.-Seven Arts. Vincent McEveety, director. With James Stewart, Inger Stevens, Gary Lockwood, Dean Jagger, Ed Begley, Barbara Luna, Jack Elam. This moody Western pits Fonda, as a gang leader, against Stewart's town sheriff.

Yours, Mine and Ours (1968), United Artists. Melville Shavelson, director. With Lucille Ball, Van Johnson, Tom Bosley. Widower and widow combine families—eighteen kids!—in a story that rises above the predictable.

Madigan (1968), Universal. Don Siegel, director. With Richard Widmark, Michael Dunn, Inger Stevens, Harry Guardino, James Whitmore, Susan Clark, Raymond S. Jacques, Sheree North. Fonda plays a priggish commissioner riding herd over Widmark's detective in this taut police psychodrama.

The Boston Strangler (1968), Twentieth Century-Fox. Richard Fleischer, director. With Tony Curtis, George Kennedy, Mike Kellin, Murray Hamilton, Hurd Hatfield, Sally Kellerman. Flashy treatment of the mid-1960s Boston psychopath, with Fonda the pursuer.

Once Upon a Time in the West (1969), Paramount. Sergio Leone, director. With Claudia Cardinale, Jason Robards, Gabriele Ferzetti, Charles Bronson, Keenan Wynn, Jack Elam, Woody Strode. Stylized Western violence in the Sergio Leone mode, with Fonda startling audiences with his supervillainous role.

Too Late the Hero (1970), Cinerama. Robert Aldrich, director. With Michael Caine, Cliff Robertson. Fonda plays a brief scene as a World War II army captain in the Pacific.

There Was a Crooked Man (1970), Warner Bros.-Seven Arts. Joseph L. Mankiewicz, director. With Kirk Douglas, Hume Cronyn, Warren Oates, Burgess Meredith, Lee Grant. Fonda as a fast-gun-turned-prison-warden who prevents escape of murderer Kirk Douglas.

Opposite: Fonda on location in Kernville, Oregon, in June 1970 for the film *Sometimes a Great Notion*. Fonda portrays a logger in the film, which was based on a novel by Ken Kesey and was filmed on Oregon's Siletz River.

Henry Fonda, at left, in another scene from the film, directed by Jack Smight.

Midway, filmed in 1975, tells of the U.S. Navy's efforts in the Pacific during World War II. Fonda, at left, portrays Adm. Chester Nimitz, commander of the U.S. Pacific Fleet during the war. Also appearing in the film were Glenn Ford, center, as Adm. Spruance, and Robert Mitchum as Adm. Bull Halsey.

The Cheyenne Social Club (1970), National General. Gene Kelly, director. With James Stewart, Shirley Jones, Sue Ann Langdon. Comedy Western in which two cowboys inherit a brothel.

Sometimes a Great Notion (1971), Universal. Paul Newman, director. With Paul Newman, Lee Remick, Michael Sarrazin, Richard Jaeckel. Fonda plays the patriarch of a family of Oregon lumberjacks. Excellent action and locations, and Oscar nominations for Jaeckel as Best Supporting Actor and for Alan and Marilyn Bergman's song (music by Henry Mancini).

The Serpent (1972), Les Films La Boetie. Henri Verneuil, director. With Yul Brynner, Dirk Bogarde, Philippe Noiret, Michel Bouquet, Farley Granger, Virna Lisi. Fonda plays a CIA director in this story of a Russian secret police colonel (Brynner) who defects to the West.

Ash Wednesday (1973), Paramount. Larry Peerce, director. With Elizabeth Taylor, Helmut Berger, Keith Baxter, Maurice Teynac, Margaret Blye. Elizabeth Taylor, as

Fonda's wife, gets a head-to-toe facelift to try to reattract Fonda. The critics thought the European locales looked great and little else.

My Name Is Nobody (1973), Universal. Tonino Valerii, director. With Terence Hill, Jean Martin, Piero Lulli, Leo Gordon, R. G. Armstrong, Neil Summers. Billed as a presentation by spaghetti Western king Sergio Leone, this stylish cowboy yarn featured Fonda as Jack Beauregard, the Old West's greatest surviving gun slinger. Beauregard, hoping to retire in peace in Europe, is goaded by Nobody (Hill) into one more big fight. His opponents: 150 members of the notorious Wild Bunch. The critics said it was clichéd but entertaining.

Midway (1976), Universal. Jack Smight, director. With Charlton Heston, Robert Mitchum, Glenn Ford, Edward Albert, Toshiro Mifune, Robert Wagner, James Coburn, Hal Holbrook. Fonda in a small role in an all-star spectacular, this time as Admiral Nimitz, commander of U.S. forces in the Pacific in the 1942 Battle of Midway.

Fonda, with costar Michael Caine, in a scene from
Irwin Allen's 1977 production of *The Swarm*. Fonda
plays an immunologist brought in to help fight an
invasion of African killer bees.

Fonda with the rest of the cast from *The Swarm*.
From left, Bradford Dillman, Fonda, Caine,
Katharine Ross, producer Allen, Olivia De Havilland,
Fred MacMurray, Richard Widmark, Richard
Chamberlain.

Rollercoaster (1977), Universal. James Goldstone, director. With George Segal, Richard Widmark, Timothy Bottoms, Susan Strasberg, Harry Guardino. Fonda makes a cameo as a security expert trying to deal with a pyrotechnics expert who is holding an amusement park for ransom.

Tentacles (1977), American International Pictures, Twentieth Century-Fox. Oliver Hellman (a.k.a. Ovidio Assonitis), director. With John Huston, Shelley Winters, Bo Hopkins, Cesare Danova, Claude Akins. Two killer whales are trained to destroy a giant octopus that menaces the southern California coast. Fonda has a few walk-ons as the head of a marine tunneling outfit that literally digs up the creature.

The Great Smokey Roadblock (also **The Last of the Cowboys**) (1977), Blowitz & Canton. John Leone, director. With Eileen Brennan, Robert Englund, John Byner, Austin Pendleton, Susan Sarandon, Melanie Mayron. Fonda, a trucker terminally ill with cancer, steals back his repossessed eighteen-wheeler and highballs it across the United States in one last run. He is aided by six prostitutes who work for an old flame (Miss Brennan).

The Swarm (1978), Warner Bros. Irwin Allen, director. With Michael Caine, Katherine Ross, Richard Widmark, Richard Chamberlain, Fred MacMurray, Olivia De Havilland, Ben Johnson, José Ferrer, Lee Grant, Slim Pickens. Fonda plays an immunologist brought in to help fight an invasion of African killer bees.

Fedora (1978), Rialto Films. Billy Wilder, director. With Marthe Keller, William Holden, José Ferrer, Hildegard Knef, Frances Sternhagen, Michael York. In a small role,

Fonda plays himself as the head of the motion picture academy bestowing an Oscar on Fedora (Miss Keller).

Meteor (1979). American International Pictures. Ronald Neame, director. With Sean Connery, Natalie Wood, Karl Malden, Brian Keith, Martin Landau, Trevor Howard, Richard Dysart, Joseph Campanella. As the U.S. president, Fonda and the Russians try to divert a giant asteroid on a collision course with New York City.

City on Fire (1979), Avco Embassy. Alvin Rakoff, director. With Barry Newman, Susan Clark, Shelley Winters, Leslie Nielsen, James Franciscus, Ava Gardner. Fonda is a fire chief faced with a disgruntled ex-refinery worker who douses the city with gasoline and lights a match.

Wanda Nevada (1979), United Artists. Peter Fonda, director. With Peter Fonda, Brooke Shields. Fonda plays a

bit part as a prospector for his son, who produced as well as directed this pay television film.

Battle of Mareth (1979), Dimension. (Also known as **The Greatest Battle**.) Orson Welles, narrator. With Helmut Berger, Samantha Eggar, John Huston, Stacy Keach. A film about WWII in which Fonda plays a general.

On Golden Pond (1981), Universal. Mark Rydell, director. With Katharine Hepburn, Jane Fonda, Dabney Coleman, Doug McKeon. Fonda and Hepburn, as aging Norman and Ethel Thayer, return to their favorite Golden Pond for what probably will be their last summer together. A marvelous story, marvelously done. Fonda's one and only acting Oscar. (Katharine Hepburn won the Best Actress Academy Award.)

Opposite, below, and following pages:
Scenes from the critically acclaimed box-office hit *On Golden Pond*, directed by Mark Rydell, and released by Universal in 1981. It was Henry Fonda's last major role and the only movie for which he won an Academy Award, as Best Actor for his role as the aging Norman Thayer. Katharine Hepburn, who also won an Oscar for her performance, played his wife, Ethel. Fonda's daughter, Jane, appeared as their daughter Chelsea in a role that echoed some of the difficult real-life emotions that the two felt for each other. Doug McKeon played the role of Chelsea's stepson. For Henry Fonda, it was a final performance of great depth and perception, the kind of acting that over the decades became his trademark and made him one of America's most accomplished and beloved actors.